The Keys
to
Successful Recruiting and Staffing

by
Barry Siegel

WEDDLE's
www.weddles.com
2052 Shippan Avenue
Stamford, CT 06902

To my beautiful wife, Bobbie ...
my all time greatest and most challenging recruit.

Table of Contents

Forward

Why read a book about recruiting and staffing when the economy is slow, and candidates are in seemingly endless supply? Indeed, who needs to worry about recruitment at all now that the War for Talent is over?

Such questions are common place these days. They are rooted in the traditional view of recruitment as a labor faucet that can easily and quickly be turned on and provide an endless supply of talent at the exact time and in the exact place it's needed. It is a buyer's market, after all; people are chasing jobs, so all recruiters need to do is let workers know that jobs are available, and they'll show up, resume in hand. Despite the recession that began in 2000, adherence to this view is a recipe for corporate disaster. The labor shortages that caused the War for Talent to break out in the mid 1990's are becoming even more prevalent today. But that's not the most important reason why Corporate America needs to place a greater priority on recruiting and staffing.

We live in a time of irony. Companies now invest tens of millions of dollars in building and promoting their product and service brands, yet they invest little or nothing at all in the principal delivery system for those brands: people. Whether they are multinational conglomerates or local retailers, companies know that their success, in large measure, turns on the power of their brand. So, it is ironic, but also dangerous that many of those same companies ignore the very people who will make that brand what it is.

Think of it this way: people deliver the brand that marketing builds. They shape it, service it, and renew it with every action they take and every response they make. Whenever a customer walks into a showroom, a café, a hospital or a store, it's their interaction with the employees of that company that will determine the fate of its brand. In effect, the attributes of those employees—their skills, commitment, attitude—become the attributes of the brand. They are its personification. If they fall short, the brand is diminished, as well.

Talent matters, therefore, because brands matter. And what matters most—for brands as well as talent—is quality. Effective talent management is not about hiring more people; it's about hiring the right people. Fundamentally, it's an exercise in getting the right people at the right time for the right job. That's the only way a brand can be delivered effectively—by quality people who love their jobs and do the best they can day-in, day-out for their employers.

That's the subject of this book. Making smart investments in talent acquisition is what *The Keys to Successful Recruiting and Staffing* is all about. Barry Siegel has drawn on his 30+ years of experience to craft a roadmap for organizations that realize the importance of preparing now for the competition they will face for top talent in the future. Those that follow his advice will be well positioned to compete for the best talent and, as a consequence, better able to implement brands with power and distinction.

Alan V. Schwartz
CEO, Bernard Hodes Group

About the Author

Barry Siegel
Bernard Hodes Group
President, Interactive and Staffing Solutions
President, Recruitment Enhancement Services

Barry Siegel has been in the recruitment field since 1970, and has been with Bernard Hodes Group since 1971. After holding virtually every account service, creative and management position within the organization, and founding the company, Recruitment Enhancement Services, he was promoted in January, 2002, to President, Interactive and Staffing Solutions.

Barry holds a BS in Business Management from Fairleigh Dickinson University and has been a member of Who's Who Worldwide, and is a lifetime member of America's Registry of Outstanding Professionals. A recognized innovator and authority on cost effective recruiting, Barry has authored numerous online articles and a chapter on recruitment outsourcing in *On Staffing: Advice and Perspectives*, as well as his present book, *The Keys to Successful Recruiting and Staffing*. He has been a featured speaker at major meetings of numerous professional organizations, including the Employment Management Association, Society for Human Resource Management, International Quality & Productivity Center and the Bureau of National Affairs. The November, 2002 issue of *Human Resources Outsourcing Today* recognized Barry as having "invented recruitment process outsourcing," and named him among "The 100 Superstars of HR Outsourcing."

Introduction

During the mid-to-late 1990's, the recruiting and staffing function in large and small corporate enterprises moved from the back office to the center stage of business. The paradigm shift of this post-1995 era was caused primarily by the fact that there were too many jobs available for too few qualified people. All of a sudden, sourcing and retaining talent were finally recognized as major contributors to an organization's future and overall net worth. Millions of dollars were invested as Corporate America mobilized in an effort to win their unique War for Talent. They built "war rooms" fortified with state-of-the-art technology and staffed with Internet sourcing specialists. Many valuable lessons were learned in the process.

Then, along came the recession of the early 2000s and many of those valuable lessons were somehow forgotten. Countless organizations abandoned their newly constructed talent acquisition war rooms in favor of cutting headcount in order to meet short term budgetary constraints. But the staffing function did not return to the back office. On the contrary, it remains today in the spotlight, but under a microscope.

In addition, the demographics strongly indicate that a new War for Talent is about to emerge. And that reality presents you with a clear choice: You can wait for a surprise attack of requisitions for new hires flying in from all directions, or you can wage a preemptive strike by immediately focusing on a comprehensive, proactive strategy for success.

This book presents a battle plan for those who opt to pursue the latter course. As shown below, it is composed of one rule of thumb and a number of keys organized into the four key sets that can open your organization to successful recruiting and staffing in the post-1995 era.

RULE OF THUMB: The People You Are Looking
For, Probably Aren't Looking
For You!

KEYSETS:

- **Key Set #1:**   Becoming an Employer of Choice

- **Key Set #2:**   The Cycle of Response and Responsiveness

- **Key Set #3:**   It's All in the Marketing Mix

- **Key Set #4:**   Flexibility and Hiring for a Culture Fit

Rather than viewing these keys and key sets as simple tools designed to open the door to greater staffing success on their own, visualize them in combinations, similar to the key sets required to open a safe. Your degree of success will be dependent upon:

- when you use each key;

- how you use each key; and

- the particular order and sequence of the specific keys you use.

More importantly, no key, key set, or combination of keys will work unless you truly believe that "the people you are looking for, probably aren't looking for you." The good old days when luck, chance, and osmosis caused great candidates to show up at your door whenever you needed them are gone forever. This book is all about adjusting to that reality, and equally as important, using that adjustment to gain a competitive advantage in your staffing efforts.

Why should you believe that these keys will work in your particular situation? That's a very good question. One of my most strongly held convictions is that people should become familiar enough with a subject to reach a level of competence where they at least "know what they don't know." I know that I don't know your particular situation. But, the odds are that I have seen at least one situation similar to yours, and you may be able to benefit from that experience.

I began my career in recruitment with a firm in New York called Diener and Dorskind Advertising back in 1970. In 1971, I joined Bernard Hodes Advertising in New York, and in 1977, moved to Houston, Texas to head up that agency's local branch office. I was eager to go to Houston because I was tired of dealing with recessions and was told that the city was "recession proof," thanks to the strength of the oil industry. Well, Houston might have been "recession proof," but just five years later, it went from "boom-town USA" to the worst "depression" I'd ever seen.

The Houston of that boom period (from 1977-1981) was a preview of what the rest of the country would experience from 1996-2000: too many jobs and too few qualified people to fill them. And when the bottom dropped out in Houston in 1982, the challenges we faced were much like those experienced by the rest of the nation in the recession of the early 2000s. Not only did our clients stop running recruitment ads, but our contacts at those companies were laid off because hiring came to a dead stop. We decided to seize the opportunity to hire some of those former clients and find a way to combine their Human Resource expertise with the recruitment marketing expertise of our Houston office. This new capability, which we called Recruitment Enhancement Services or RES, enabled us to service clients with recruiting needs in other parts of the country. It both ensured our survival and launched an elementary form of recruitment outsourcing ... long before it became fashionable.

Today, I remain with that same organization, which is now known as Bernard Hodes Group (Hodes). It is recognized as North America's foremost provider of recruitment communications and staffing solutions. And from that crisis-driven beginning, Recruitment Enhancement Services (RES) has emerged as a leader in the recruitment outsourcing field.

Over the course of 30+ years, I've personally been involved with many hundreds of recruiting situations, on behalf of clients, and observed thousands of others. When you last this long in the same industry, you certainly experience your fair share of failure. In my view, however, the secret to success is not avoiding failure, but learning from it.

I believe it was Edison who considered each time he failed in his attempt to invent the light bulb as a discovery of one more way the light bulb would not be invented. Well, I've tried and seen thousands of ways NOT to be successful at recruiting. I've also witnessed and been a part of just as many or more success stories. When you are involved with such a wide variety of recruitment activity, patterns begin to emerge. Those patterns are the key sets and keys described in this book. My hope is that they will not only permit you to learn from the successes I've experienced, but also prevent you from repeating the errors I've made and observed throughout my long career.

Barry Siegel
Houston, Texas

Chapter 1

Key Set #1
Becoming an Employer of Choice

World class recruiting and staffing organizations set themselves apart through their ability to attract and retain champions, people who are eager to step forward and spread the gospel about life on-the-job. Their joys are real, their sales pitches earnest.

Employees of top-flight organizations love to "sell" the company that is their employer, and what makes them do that is no great mystery: In a tight labor market, these organizations make it their business to win over every potential recruit by becoming – and remaining – "an employer of choice."

Is your organization an employer of choice? If you're not sure, ask yourself the following questions:

- Does your company avoid policies and procedures that make it difficult to find and keep the kind of employees it most wants and needs?

- Does your organization allocate the time, money and additional resources needed to find and keep great employees?

If you can't answer both of these questions with a definite "yes," you'll have a tough time competing with today's world class recruiting and staffing organizations. According to Jim Harris and Joan Brannick in their book *Finding and Keeping Great Employees,* some companies truly believe that finding and keeping great employees is their primary challenge, and their actions support the commitment to that challenge.[1]

There are a number of specific guidelines that companies should follow if they wish to become employers of choice. The previous paragraph is a good place to start. But before further spelling out the guidelines, let's take a look at the staffing landscape in the years since 1995.

The Recruiting & Staffing Environment

The recent economic recession, which began when Internet start-ups imploded in late 2000, continues to spread fear among both employed and unemployed workers as pink slips fly and waves of layoffs continue to roll across the country. This has been a very different kind of recession, however. According to a Towers Perrin study published in late 2001,[2] the following factors were indeed unprecedented for an economic downturn:

- Despite waves of staff reductions, talent remained difficult, if not more difficult, to find;

- 73% of companies involved with layoffs were simultaneously hiring for other positions;

- More than half of all U.S. workers were still considered passive job seekers during this period, while just 12% were actually actively seeking employment elsewhere;

- 42% of the companies that were laying off employees also had targeted programs to retain top performers.

The Towers Perrin study also notes: "More recent research, including a soon-to-be-released *TP Track* study on HR, reaffirms that attracting and retaining people with critical skills remains at the top of the corporate people agenda, outdistancing even pressing cost issues, such as managing rising health care costs."[3]

Further evidence that the recession had caused a temporary cease fire rather than a true end to the War for Talent, was provided by a study of recruiting trends conducted by Kevin Wheeler in April, 2002. No less than 53.8% of the respondents to his survey projected that new professional hires would increase, and over 70% agreed that sourcing would be the most critical HR issue facing their company over the next 12 months.[4]

In addition, a nationwide survey of 16,000 businesses conducted by Manpower found that 27% of companies planned to add jobs in the third quarter of 2002, while only 8% anticipated staff cuts. When adjusted for season variations, these data reflected a 14% rise in hiring compared to the first two quarters of 2002.[5]

Despite the fact that the War Against Terror has delayed such projections for job growth, these statistics still make a great deal of sense when considered in conjunction with forecasts from the Bureau of Labor Statistics. It estimates that by the year 2006, there will be 151 million jobs in the United States while the working population will number only 141 million people. In that same year, two workers will exit the workforce for every one who enters. Workforce growth will decelerate each year from now until 2020, and the number of workers in the 25-44 year-old age bracket will decline by 15% over the next 15 years.

Against this backdrop, is it really a surprise that the staffing manager's job is now more difficult than ever? The entire recruiting and staffing landscape has changed dramatically. Mid-life career changes are commonplace. Flextime and the e-office are here to stay. Jobs come, and jobs go. By and large, loyalty to one's employer is regarded as a character flaw, or perhaps a gratuitous after-effect of corporate downsizing. Gold watches at retirement? Today's workers view them as quaint vestiges of a bygone era.

To understand how to succeed in this environment, you must first understand what has changed for staffing managers in recent years – and what hasn't. Yes, their job is tougher. But their mission is not impossible, if they appreciate the new demographic reality that confronts them and understand its impact on their job.

New Demographics

Let's look at two successive generations of job seekers:

Baby Boomers: Seventy-six million people were born between 1945 and 1964. These so-called "baby boomers" have lived through the Cold War, the Vietnam War, mega-billion dollar corporate mergers, continuous rounds of corporate downsizing and the rise and fall of instant, Internet zillionaires. We're speaking of a generation that, as a whole, feels it has shouldered more than its fair share of the load in helping to build a strong American economy. But because of their vast numbers, they could never enjoy the luxury of shopping around from job-to-job. In spite of their increasingly skeptical attitude toward corporate America, they still largely feel the need to demonstrate long-term commitment to their employers.

Baby Busters: Baby boomers had far fewer children than their parents. Some 65 million people—the generation of so-called "baby busters"—were born between 1965 and 1984. That's 11 million fewer people than their parents' generation born over the same length of time! This younger generation has witnessed the Gulf War, the demise and rebirth of Apple Computer, and the son of a former President being sworn in himself as the President of the United States. More importantly and more often than not, they've seen their parents' loyalty to employers go unrewarded. As a consequence, they are determined not to repeat in their own careers the same mistakes they witnessed growing up. Fewer-in-number, they don't feel the same need to cling to one particular employer or another, the way many of their parents did. In fact, baby busters are more cynical about corporate America than their parents ever were – or could afford to be.

Who can blame them? Studies indicate that, in their parents' generation, half of a worker's job knowledge and skills became obsolete in 12-15 years. For baby busters, the competency life cycle is drastically shorter. Today, according to the U.S. Department of Labor, half of a baby buster's job skills become obsolete in just 30-36 months![6] This warp speed obsolescence is at least partially responsible for the view that baby busters are more in tune with life off the job than on it.

The challenge created by these new demographic realities has hit staffing managers hard. The talent pool has decreased by about 15 percent, causing the recruiters who work for them to scramble and shift their approach to finding talent. In the not-so-distant past, recruiters could afford to sit back and watch resumes pile up. In the post-1995 era, recruiters need to seek out recruits proactively wherever they can find them. This requirement continues today despite the fact that resume flow dramatically increased in 2001 and continues to expand even as the recession theoretically begins to recede. The problem is not the quantity of the flow, but its quality. Despite that torrent of candidate information, the flow of "qualified" resumes continues to decline due to the shrinking pool of talent.

In this environment, the most insightful organizations are redefining what recruiting and staffing means to them. Cutting-edge recruiting is no longer viewed as an administrative task that involves nothing more than picking the best candidate out of a stack of resumes on the recruiter's desk. Instead, it's seen as a sales and marketing activity with its own budget and with goals that directly contribute to the bottom line. Unfortunately, many organizations now recognize the first part of that shift, but overlook the second. As Andre Goodlett, Kellogg Company Associate Director of Staffing & Diversity, puts it, "Recruiting is nothing more than sales and marketing with a lousy budget." The honesty of that assessment, however, doesn't preclude the need to achieve recruiting results, and Andre prides himself on installing state-of-the-art processes and systems to make the most of the resume flow emanating from the budget he has to work with.

One way or another, recruiting used to "just happen." Not so anymore. In the post-1995 era, Vice Presidents of Human Resources and Chief Financial Officers are no longer so concerned with the costs of recruiting and staffing. Instead, they're trying to calculate the cost of jobs that go unfilled, the cost of attrition, and the return on their organization's recruiting investments. As a result, many staffing managers have attempted to replace traditional techniques with "magic bullets" offered by a vast array of dot.coms and their successors. These magic bullets do not exist, however, at least in the real world of the War for Talent. No matter how slick the marketing pitch, simplistic, single shot solutions do not have the power to address the challenges facing today's staffing managers. Nevertheless, the pitches continue.

Still, no matter how recruiting is defined or redefined, talented employees remain scarce and difficult to recruit. And in their quest to attract job candidates, most organizations begin on roughly the same footing. They face many of the same potential pitfalls that other employers face, regardless of the organization's size or prestige.

The tight labor market and increased global competition have turned the Human Resource professional's job into a high-stakes war for qualified applicants. Rivalries for talented IT employees became so intense between 1996-2000 that some companies made offers as soon as qualified candidates walked through the door. Such a scenario is sure to resurface shortly. But even in such an environment, with a labor market populated by baby busters averse to the notion of employer loyalty, every organization has the potential to become an employer of choice.

How can they do that? Human Resource professionals can achieve this transformation by adhering to the four recruiting and staffing keys that make up this key set:

- Develop apostles

- Leverage the power of employer branding

- Engage in market-driven behavior

- Formalize the process through marketing and automation

Let's examine each of these keys in more detail.

Key #1: Develop Apostles

This guideline is simple, but critical to recruiting success in the post-1995 era. Happy campers spread happy news or a cheerful noise. That's why so many successful organizations have gone to such great lengths to convince the world that they are excellent places to work.

One of the wonderful things about apostles is their active loyalty, a trait that can produce handsome dividends. According to a report by HR consultant Watson Wyatt Worldwide, more than half of 7,500 workers surveyed in the year 2000 said they felt committed to their employers.[7] Those companies with high worker commitment had a 112 percent, three-year return to shareholders versus a 76 percent return for firms with low worker commitment. That's the kind of dividend that will impress even the CEO.

The same study identified the following factors as crucial contributors to this feeling of commitment, and the apostle effect it encourages:

- Recruiting excellence

- Clear rewards and accountability

- A collegial, flexible workplace (management is accommodating to worker needs and everyone is addressed on a first-name basis)

- Communications integrity (shared information and input, as opposed to secrecy)

- The prudent use of resources

What makes me think I can offer advice on turning employees into apostles? Well, for one reason, I'm an apostle myself. As I mentioned earlier, I've been with the same organization—Bernard Hodes Group—for over 30 years, and I never miss an opportunity to tell anyone about what a great employer it is. No less important, I'm surrounded by apostles, not only within Bernard Hodes Group, but also within Omnicom Group, Inc., our parent company, and they, too, enjoy telling others about our organization.

This commitment or active loyalty is no accident. It's the result of hard work. For example, when you walk into the office of Tom Watson, Omnicom Group's Vice Chairman and Dean of Omnicom University, you'll see the following quote on his white board: "People join companies and leave supervisors." Dean Watson believes that recruiting success begins with retention. And retention is in the hands of the supervisor. So, employers had better make sure that their supervisors are dedicated, trained and incented to ensure that their direct reports respond affirmatively to the following questions:

- Do I know what is expected of me at work?

- Do I have the materials and equipment I need to do my work?

- Do I have the opportunity to do what I do best everyday?

- Does my supervisor, or someone at work, care about me as a person?

- At work, are my opinions listened to and given serious consideration?

These five questions are the most powerful of a list of twelve questions designed to measure the value of human capital, presented by Marcus Buckingham and Curt Coffman in their book *First Break All the Rules.*[8]

Get an affirmative answer to those five questions, and apostles become almost cult-like in their fervency. That's what good employee referral programs are all about. They leverage the proselytizing power of an employer's actively committed workers. And, if your organization exhibits the right behavior, uses an efficient recruiting and staffing process, and does effective public relations, it too will produce true believers and apostles.

Key #2: Leverage the Power of Employer Branding

Many companies won't hesitate to spend tens of millions of dollars to project the right image of a product to consumers. They have a tough time, however, parting with a dollar to project the image of the company <u>itself</u> as a great employer. It seems to me, they have it backwards. If consumers are aware that Company A is a terrific place to work, they will naturally assume that Company A produces great products. In fact, consumers will believe Company A makes great products because it is a great place to work.

In their book *The Service Profit Chain*, James Heskett, W. Earl Sasser, and Leonard Schlesinger describe a logic that boils down to this: "Service profit chain thinking maintains that there are direct and strong relationships between profit; growth; customer loyalty; customer satisfaction; the value of goods and services delivered to customers and employee capability, satisfaction, loyalty, and productivity."[9] In other words, loyal and satisfied employees foster loyal and satisfied customers, which, in turn, results in an improved bottom line.

The service profit chain concept is justifiably getting more attention among Human Resource executives these days. It can serve as an ideal motivator and blueprint for an employer branding strategy. When companies start thinking about transforming themselves into great places to work and then project that image to external candidates and their own employees, they'll attract and motivate great workers. These happy workers—who are often apostles—will do the best possible job of taking care of customers, and that, in turn, will take care of the bottom line. Which is another way of saying: Great people make great companies. Simple, but profoundly true.

Key #3: Engage in Market-Driven Behavior

Five-to-ten years ago, companies liked to feel as if they were in total control, on top of a tight job market. They often assumed a position of advantage in job interviews, forcing the candidate to do the selling. That changed in the post-1995 era, when conventional laws of supply and demand forced changes in behavior among knowing employers. But, some companies, bolstered by the tidal wave of resumes generated by a slow economic recovery from the recession of the early 2000s, have made the mistake of returning to this antiquated technique. The knowing employer, on the other hand, recognizes that the demographics haven't changed, and it is they that must do the selling. Otherwise, the candidates they can't afford to lose may walk out the door and across the street to their competitor.

The HR Director of a Fortune 500 company offers this perspective on the new balance of power between employer and job seeker: "You wouldn't call on your customers and say, 'So tell me, how are you qualified to buy my product?' So, why give job candidates the third degree?" He rightly concludes: "They're as valuable to a company as the next customer."

In the past, all job candidates, without exception, were required to apply in writing with a resume and cover letter sent via regular mail. These days, the market demands that candidates be able to reach recruiters at any time of day or night that they—the candidates—want to do so. A good corporate Web-site enables them to do just that. To be effective, therefore, recruiters must be in perpetual motion. The most successful recruiters make themselves available 24 hours/day, 7 days/week to answer candidates' questions via e-mail, telephone, or in-person. They understand that if they don't reach out to candidates, someone else will. In addition, well conceived Internet capabilities strengthen the organization's capacity to provide candidates with around-the-clock access.

Why is such access necessary? Consider the retail industry. It has always understood that most sales occur on weekends and responded to this market imperative accordingly. Hence, retailers staff up for weekend customers. Similarly, weekdays, from 9-5, are when the vast majority of qualified candidates are busy at their current jobs and unable to respond to recruiters. Thus, the market commands that prospective employers make themselves available to job prospects at the job prospects' convenience – lunchtime, evenings, weekends.

In effect, this key puts candidates in charge. "When customers see a TV commercial for a product they want, they should be able to call a toll-free telephone number or go online to order it whenever they want," an HR Vice President said recently. "It's virtually the same process for talented job candidates."

Key #4: Formalize the Process Through Marketing and Automation

In an earlier era, much of the recruiting and staffing process was judged by weight and bulk. In other words, a recruiting program was deemed successful if it generated a stack of resumes and reams of letters from job-seeking candidates. The higher the pile of paper on a recruitment manager's desk, the more effective the process was considered. All of that has now changed. World-class recruiting and staffing operations are no longer paper-weight driven. They are, instead, Internet-enabled and, to a large degree, automated.

Being automated, however, doesn't translate into sitting back and watching the process take care of itself. No longer are recruiters responsible simply for eliminating candidates. In fact, the best job candidates don't just come knocking anymore. Recruiters must seek them out and sell them on their employer's opportunity. In the past, resumes would flow in with relatively little effort on the recruiter's part. Recruiters in the post-1995 era, on the other hand, must take a proactive marketing approach. If an opening is not filled, the Human Resources department will take the blame, even if the company itself is at fault for not providing the proper resources (e.g., expecting HR generalists to get the recruiting job done in addition to all of their other responsibilities).

In addition, the recruitment and staffing process needs to be automated in such a way that many of these core responsibilities can be easily and efficiently handled. The task of applying for a job, for example, must leverage automation to allow for online applications. For many organizations, automation entails online job postings. Some also engage in Internet-based interviewing, in which online questions are posed to candidates. Based on the answers, the employer's candidate management system automatically ranks candidates.

An effective, automated process also produces another valuable benefit: metrics. Top recruiting and staffing organizations can generate data in nanoseconds. At any time, these companies can create the information needed to measure such areas as recruitment costs, time-to-fill, and customer satisfaction. But automation alone will not produce optimum recruiting performance. It must be combined with the human touch of marketing. In short, recruiting and staffing remains a people business.

A Winning Formula

Even in a labor market where employer loyalty is widely assumed to be a thing of the past, every organization has the potential to become an employer of choice, one of the four essential "key sets" that characterize a world-class recruiting and staffing organization. By using all of the time-tested keys in the set, employers will achieve true and lasting success.

Chapter 2

Key Set #2
The Cycle of Response and Responsiveness

There's no disputing that every company goes through similar steps during the hiring process, steps that I call the "cycle of response and responsiveness." Recruiting is a team effort involving candidates, recruiters, hiring managers, third parties, support staff, and even your marketing and IT departments. What sets one company apart from another is how effectively all of the parties involved in the process respond and are responsive to each other.

There's a truism in sports that is applicable to staffing, as well. With very rare exceptions, the winning team is the one where the whole exceeds the sum of the parts. Similarly, to be successful in recruiting and staffing, you need to assemble an assortment of "specialists" and get them to work together as a team, rather than as a loose-knit bunch of individuals.

The first step, of course, is to identify and "recruit" the members of the "recruiting" team. Who are the members of that team? Well, it's obvious that you start with high caliber recruiters. But, a recruiting team must have more than recruiters to be successful. Let's compare it to a baseball team. If recruiting were a baseball team, recruiters would probably be the pitchers. Can you imagine fielding a baseball team of all pitchers? How many pitchers can hit? And, did you ever see a pitcher willing to be a catcher? Probably not. So, that means we need hitters and a catcher. Now, let's focus on the catcher for a minute. Who in the recruiting and staffing organization is going to be the catcher? It will probably be someone in HR management, say the staffing manager or the Director of HR. They are the people who "catch" most of the heat, if the pitching (recruiting) staff doesn't get the job done.

Having found a pitcher and catcher, we have our battery, but who's going to play first base? There is no game until a hiring manager comes up with a need, so I'd have to say that the hiring manager should take first. Second base can then be covered by the hiring manager's support staff. Why is that appropriate? Because if we can't get information and feedback from the hiring manager, we can't play ball. So, whether it's a secretary, administrative assistant or associate to the hiring manager … we need people at second base who can cover first when the hiring manager is unavailable. Once that important position is filled, we can move over to third base. The best people to fill that position are the third party vendors that support your recruiting and staffing function. These might include your recruitment ad agency, temporary staffing agencies, employment agencies, search firms, the people who check references and backgrounds, any testing agencies, and anyone else to whom you outsource any aspect of staffing operations.

That rounds out our infield, with one important exception. Who's going to play shortstop? In many cases, it's the shortstop who is the glue that holds any great team together. And the shortstop in the recruiting and staffing organization has got to be the receptionist. Receptionists set the tone and make the first impression.

They make a candidate feel either at home or unwelcome, just by the tone in their voice. Without a great receptionist who's quick on their feet, any company is going to have a tough time achieving recruiting success. If you don't believe me, place an anonymous call to your own company pretending to be an ideal candidate who possesses perfect qualifications for a position you're having a difficult time filling. How does the experience make you feel? Do you want to work for your company or move on to the competition?

OK, we've got all the bases covered ... recruiters, HR management, the hiring manager, the hiring manager's support staff, third party vendors and the receptionist. Now, all we have to do is get them to work hard together, and recruiting will be a cinch, right? WRONG. Did you ever see a baseball team win without an outfield? Of course not. So, who will play the outfield in the recruiting process? In the previous chapter, I noted that one of the keys for success was engaging in market-driven behavior. To do so, however, you need a strong marketing department, one that understands the importance of recruiting; one that embraces the concept of employer branding. That kind of marketing department is a team player and perfect for your left fielder.

Next comes centerfield; who should play there? Remember the fourth key in the last chapter? It was to formalize the recruiting process through marketing and automation. Now, you've already got marketing in left field, so how do you get automation into the game? How do you get career Web-sites and applicant tracking systems on your team? To do that, you'll need cooperation and buy-in from the IT department. So, that group is your center fielder.

Who, then, are we going to get to cover right field? The right fielder is usually the person with the strongest arm on the team. They can nail just about anyone trying to steal an extra base on them. Who plays that role in most companies? You guessed it. The Finance department is your right fielder. Championships are won by teams that focus on recruiting, motivating, and retaining the best players. Has any team where the priority was cost cutting ever won the World Series? Of course not. Therefore, if a recruiting organization wants to be a world champion (and what recruiting organization doesn't?), it needs a Finance department that focuses on return on investment, rather than on shopping for the so-called "best deal."

We've now filled all of the positions, so what's left to complete our recruiting and staffing team? How about the most important player of all ... the candidate? They're your designated hitter. Only a successful candidate can get you a home run. Add them to the team, and you've got a full complement of 10 players, so let's play ball!

But wait, there's still a problem. You can't play winning baseball without the people who tell the players where, when and for how much to play. That means you need a coaching staff, to make sure the team is prepared for every game. The coaching staff is your company's top management. They, in turn, work through an on-field manager who actually calls the shots. And, in the game of recruiting and staffing, the manager is the top HR person in the organization, the Vice President of Human Resources. But, the manager can only be successful with the support of the general manager. In the recruiting game, this role is played by the CEO. And finally, every team has an owner or owners for whom they must produce. For a company's recruiting and staffing organization, of course, the ultimate owners are the stockholders. And how well, or how poorly, the organization recruits has a direct effect on the performance of the company and, hence, on the long term value of the owners' stock in the company.

So, there you have it: a fully fielded recruiting and staffing team. With that in place, we're ready to PLAY BALL!

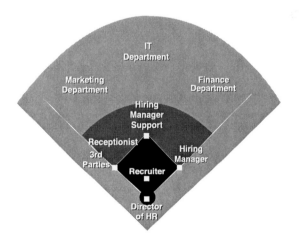

Designated Hitter: Candidate
Coaching Staff: Top Management
Manager: VPHR

General Manager: CEO
Owner: Stockholders

Now that we have our recruiting team together, it's time to discuss the ground rules of the game. I'm not talking about the rules of baseball, however. I want to focus, instead, on the hiring process. The steps in this process are described in the diagram below. I call it "The Cycle of Response and Responsiveness."

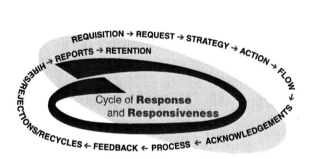

While demographics have shifted the dynamics of recruiting, the hiring process itself hasn't changed at all … and doesn't seem likely to, any time soon. In almost any company, the typical chain of events still begins when someone quits or is fired, or the workload expands and additional staff must be hired. From that point on, every organization goes through a similar process or series of steps. A requisition is completed to obtain (a) permission to fill the opening and (b) a strategy for how to go about filling it. With the requisition's approval, that strategy is implemented to generate a flow of candidates. The candidates enter a process that eventually results in an interview for those who are determined to be most qualified. Finally, one person is selected. The recruiting organization then gathers feedback on the results of the hiring process, including rejections, recycles, and hires, and the company compiles reports based upon these data. At the very end, but most importantly, the process of retention begins for those who have been hired.

The words most often associated with this process tend to be variations of the verb "respond." Nothing happens if a candidate does not "respond" to a job offering. No hire can be made if a hiring manager is not "responsive" to the recruiter's requests to set up face-to-face interviews with qualified candidates. What, then, makes one company more successful than another when it comes to the hiring process? Assuming all other factors are equal, it is the degree to which the individual participants in the process are "responsive" to one another's requests, and the relative user friendliness of the system that is supposed to facilitate their "responsiveness" to such requests.

The following table identifies each step in the hiring process and illustrates both "unresponsive" and "best practices" in implementing them. While the process may differ slightly from one organization to another, all companies—big and small—go through these or similar steps when hiring. What differentiates a successful recruiting team from the rest of the pack is the caliber of the practices implemented by the members of the team. High caliber practices and mutual respect allow the whole to exceed the sum of the responses.

UNRESPONSIVE PRACTICES	BEST PRACTICES
a. Requisition:	
Offline form	Online form
No database of previous requisition content	Database filled with job titles, descriptions, and other pertinent information
b. Request for Approval of Requisition:	
No formal approval system exists	There is an automated approval system that is easy to understand and use
The approval process is complex	
c. Strategy for Filling Requisition:	
Hiring manager is left to own devices	Automated system informs internal experts and/or appropriate third party recruiting organizations
Internal experts and/or third party recruiting organizations not easily accessible	
Numerous third party recruiters are used and treated as "vendors"	A small core group of third party recruiters are utilized as "partners"

UNRESPONSIVE PRACTICES	BEST PRACTICES
c. Strategy for Filling Requisition (con't):	
Records of previous recruiting strategies are unavailable	The recruiting strategy selected for each opening is based upon sound research
Company is unwilling to try anything new	Company is willing to try something new
d. Action:	
Hiring manager or HR is left to own devices to execute the selected strategy	Process is in place to implement the selected strategy easily
Rigid procedures are specified for responding to the job opening (written resume via snail mail is the only acceptable way to apply)	Responses for a job opening are accepted online or via phone 24/7
e. Candidate Resume/Information Flow:	
There is no formal system for processing candidate responses	There is an automated system in place for processing and screening candidates
There is no automated database in which candidate resumes/information can be stored and/or updated	There is an automated database of candidate resumes/information that is kept up-to-date and which recruiters can access easily
f. Acknowledgements:	
No formal process is in place	Automated acknowledgements are built into the system and easy to use
The process is so rigid and complex that it's not used	
g. Interview Process:	
No formal process is in place	Consistent process calls for a telephone interview of qualified candidates, within 48 hours of initial response, followed by face-to-face interviews with no more than 3 individuals, within a 30 day period.
The process in place is rigid, time consuming and imposes on candidates' dignity	
Application forms are available only as hard copy and are not included in a candidate's electronic file	Application forms are available online and become a part of the candidate's electronic file

UNRESPONSIVE PRACTICES	BEST PRACTICES
h. Feedback:	
No formal process is in place to track activities associated with each candidate	Online system tracks each step of the process for each candidate.
There are no set deadlines and/or responsibilities for providing feedback about applicants	The system requires an action within a specified timeline and identifies those who do not meet the deadline
i. Hires/Rejections/Recycles:	
Hiring manager is left to own devices	All candidate information remains in the organization's database for future consideration across all positions
No system is in place to refer candidates for other positions within the organization or to cultivate an ongoing relationship with them	An automated relationship marketing system is in place to send periodic messages to candidates in the database
No system is in place to debrief applicants who are offered jobs	System requires debriefing of all applicants who are offered jobs
j. Reports:	
No formal process is in place to generate reports on hiring activity	A wide variety of reports are available and easily generated within the system
Reports are available but very difficult to access within the system	The report data are used to identify and implement process improvements
More time is spent preparing reports than on actual recruiting	
k. Retention:	
There is an informal or awkward on-boarding process	The on-boarding process is well defined and administered
There is an informal or poorly administered employee referral program	There is a well administered online employee referral program
There is an informal or poorly administered internal mobility system	There is a well administered online internal mobility system
There is an informal exit interview process or none exists	A formal exit interview process is in place

Hypothetical Examples

In order to illustrate the points made in the preceding table, I've provided the following two examples. One illustrates a hiring process that uses "unresponsive practices," while the other illustrates a process utilizing "best practices."

A. A Hiring Process With "Unresponsive Practices"

Al Jenkins, a software development engineer with 15 years experience (internally classified as an "Engineer III"), resigns from XYZ Company. In addition to his other responsibilities, Al has been helping to build an in-house system to allow candidates to apply for jobs online. This project was initiated because the company turned down a proposal from an Application Service Provider (an Internet-based vendor) to furnish a complete hiring management system. The system was rejected because the internal IT department insists that all candidate applications reside on XYZ Company servers, and the Finance department does not approve of paying third party vendors for services that can, at least in theory, be performed in-house. Al's supervisor, of course, needs to replace Al, but isn't quite sure what to do. He decides to worry about paperwork later and calls his friend at the search firm who placed him with the XYZ Company. He asks him to begin searching for candidates. The Company Human Resource department, on the other hand, wants to begin its own candidate sourcing efforts, so it sends the hiring manager a requisition form. The hiring manager really has no precedent or guidelines to follow, so he fills out the form without giving it much thought. After all, his friend at the search firm has the opening covered.

Four weeks go by, and nothing has happened. The hiring manager calls the search firm and discovers that his friend is no longer employed there. In a panic, he calls the internal HR department to see if they have any candidates. The recruiting manager tells him that the requisition has not been approved by the hiring manager's boss. That puts the hiring manager in the difficult position of having to explain to his boss that he needs approval for making a hire that his boss thought had already been made. He gets through that meeting, however, and with signature in hand, the hiring manager goes back to HR and demands immediate service.

With no time to develop a sensible recruiting strategy and no ability to accept online responses from candidates, the HR department puts an ad in the local newspaper. The ad reads:

> "Engineer III with 15 years experience,
> mail your resume to P.O. Box 123, *Daily Herald*."

HR decides not to identify the company in the ad because it doesn't understand the new graphic standards published by the Marketing department and doesn't want to get into trouble for not properly displaying the company's logo. What they've forgotten is that the best candidates usually won't answer blind ads because they're afraid that they might be responding to their own employers. In addition, top prospects often don't have an updated resume so they have nothing to send in, and no way to contact the company.

The resumes from the candidates who do respond don't get to HR until 7 days after the ad has appeared because they go to the newspaper before being forwarded. Fifty responses come in, but most are from a wide variety of engineers who do not qualify because they are unaware that an "Engineer III" at the XYZ Company is involved in software development. Although there were four responses from software developers, HR disqualifies three because each has only 3-5 years experience, and the opening requires 15 years experience. An HR generalist conducts a telephone interview with the remaining software developer who appears to be a fit; that person is invited in for a face-to-face interview. Another week passes before the hiring manager sees this candidate and concludes that she does not have the requisite experience with JAVA and active server pages to do the job. Unfortunately, the HR generalist had not been aware of these requirements because they were not noted on the requisition.

The generalist then shows the hiring manager the three responses that had been disqualified because the candidates only had 3-5 years experience (note: JAVA hasn't been around for 15 years). The hiring manager says, "These three are perfect, invite them in." HR then discovers, however, that two of them are no longer on the market. The third, Mary Jones, is invited in, but she's new to the area (her husband has just been relocated to take a new job) and gets lost on the way to the appointment. Desperate, she calls the company's main number only to have the receptionist say, "I'm too busy to give directions right now, call back later."

Despite that setback, Mary Jones is patient enough to come back for four interviews with four different individuals over the next four weeks. (She needs the extra time to get her new house in order.) She turns out to be an ideal candidate and is finally made an offer and accepts. She reports to work two weeks later, excited about the work she will be doing in her new position. Unfortunately, her desk and computer don't arrive until the week later.

Meanwhile, the hiring manager receives an invoice from the search firm. It seems they had gone ahead with the search that was originally phoned into the hiring manager's friend. By coincidence, they too had referred Mary Jones for the opening and were now looking to collect a placement fee. The hiring manager had never seen Mary's resume or any resumes, for that matter, arrive from the search firm. He asks his assistant if she's seen any resumes, and she replies, "None except for a

Mary Jones, but doesn't she already work here?" Not long after that, Mary Jones resigns to take a job with UVW, Inc., and XYZ has to start the recruiting process all over again.

B. A Hiring Process With "Best Practices"

UVW, Inc. is an employer with a well designed and carefully implemented hiring process. When there is a need to recruit new employees, hiring managers go online and fill out a user-friendly requisition, complete with help screens and pull-down menus. The system also provides an automated search of the firm's candidate database, as well as a built-in approval process that initially posts the new job on the company's intranet. If the position is not filled within a week, the requisition is "pushed" to the third party partner organization for the development of alternative recruiting strategies. These strategies are used to supplement the standard recruitment marketing campaign that is always underway in the company.

It was this standard campaign that caught the interest of Al Jenkins several months ago. Having been assigned to work on a poorly defined and ever-changing hiring management system in addition to his normal everyday tasks, he felt overburdened. So, while he was online one day, he responded to a banner ad displayed on a niche site and was linked to UVW's Web-site. Al simply clicked on an opening of interest to him, answered a few questions, and then copied and pasted his resume into the application. Within 48 hours, he was notified via e-mail that the position for which he had applied had just been filled, but that another position with slightly different requirements was opening up within a month.

Two weeks later, another questionnaire was e-mailed to Al to see if he was qualified for and interested in this new position. He responded again online and was surprised to be called for a telephone interview 24 hours later. Al was particularly impressed that HR was then able to coordinate with the hiring manager's support staff to set up simultaneous, after–hours, face-to-face interviews with three key UVW employees, including the person who would be his new boss. Even more impressive, upon his arrival at the company, the receptionist greeted him warmly and said, "You must be Mr. Jenkins, good luck with your interviews. I'm Sally Clark, don't hesitate to call me if you need anything while you're visiting us." After the interviews, an offer was made on-the-spot, and Al accepted.

Two months later, Al applied for a promotion through the company's internal mobility system. He was told that he would receive the promotion as soon as the company could find a replacement for him at his present job. His replacement at XYZ, Mary Jones, had called him several times with questions about, as well as frustrations with, the project she had inherited from him. Taking advantage of UVW's online employee referral program, Al referred Mary for his current position. The cycle of response and responsiveness was repeated, once again, only this time for Mary. She got a new job, while Al collected a referral bonus and received a nice promotion.

But that's not the end. The search firm that had sent Mary Jones' resume to XYZ, had also sent it to UVW. The resume had been sent by postal mail and was returned unopened, together with a copy of UVW's policy on third party vendors. The policy was very clear that all third party partner organizations had to be "qualified" and then were to submit their resume referrals through the same online system used by individual candidates. This particular search firm is now in the process of attempting to qualify for participation. If and when they do, a submittal of Mary Jones' resume would automatically be rejected because such a resume already exists within UVW's database. As a result, there's never any question about the payment of placement fees.

Every organization has the ability to adopt "the cycle of response and responsiveness." It simply calls for a commitment to marketing, technology, cooperation, and common sense. Yes, of course, it also requires an expenditure of time and money. But with careful controls, that investment is nowhere near as great as the cost of what companies like XYZ go through to replace employees like Al Jenkins and Mary Jones over and over again.

Good as these best practices seem in theory, it's appropriate to ask if they work in the real world. The answer to that question is an emphatic "yes." The following case study shows why. It details Kellogg

Company's use of the keys to successful recruiting and staffing. Kellogg Company chose to outsource the implementation of the keys, but they could have been executed in-house, or in a partially outsourced manner, as long as the right people, process, creativity and technology were utilized.

A Real World Example of the Winning Formula: Kellogg Company

In 1998, cereal and convenience foods manufacturer Kellogg Company had a vision to improve its recruiting function by implementing a strong vendor relationship and fully outsourcing all recruiting activities. This strategy was very much "breakthrough thinking" at that time. There were very few companies that had taken such a step, and there weren't many suppliers with demonstrated competency in providing as broad a scope of outsourcing services.

Kellogg Company was looking for a vendor that could:

- Introduce technology to improve operating efficiency;

- Provide recruiting specialists with specific areas of expertise;

- Improve performance as measured by such metrics as timeliness, quality, and diversity;

- Enhance reporting capabilities;

- Manage fluctuations in hiring volume; and

- Reduce overall recruiting costs.

The Kellogg goal was to become a world class recruiting organization – an employer of choice. Working with outsourcing partner Recruitment Enhancement Services (RES), an Omnicom Group, Inc. company, Kellogg Company followed a four-step, 360° formula to design and implement its outsourcing program. The formula, originally developed by Bernard Hodes Group, consists of four steps: Assess, Strategize, Implement, and Measure. It is described on the following pages.

Step One: ASSESS

Kellogg Company's HR leadership believed that success in the future required that they rethink the recruiting process. They understood the value of talent to Kellogg and developed a vision that would ensure the company's ability to acquire the very best people. Due to a company-wide restructuring at the end of 1998, there was a general mandate to reduce headcount and most of the recruiting staff was reassigned or released. As the company realigned and hiring needs increased, Kellogg Company began to look for a partner that could handle a variable hiring volume, provide superior technology for the recruiting function, and improve the overall effectiveness of their recruiting efforts.

When the decision was made to outsource the entire recruitment function, a strategic selection process was implemented. Kellogg used this process to narrow the list of potential vendors from 14 to one: RES, which offered a unique range of services and superior technology that met Kellogg Company's selection criteria.

Cyd Kilduff, Director of Staffing at Kellogg Company, described the process this way: "We weren't looking for an add-on; we were looking to replace an entire internal recruiting function with a supplier solution.... We were blazing a new trail in looking for a total outsourced staffing solution, not just an enhancement."

Outsourcing offered a viable way to reduce headcount while also delivering a significant improvement in quality. As Kilduff noted, cost savings were not the primary issue in the decision to outsource; rather, "We wanted the benefits of quality improvement, with the best recruitment services possible, and we wanted to get it up and running quickly."

As RES conducted its assessment of Kellogg Company's recruitment practices, it identified inconsistent processes and limited use of technology. Hiring managers around the country were using over 80 different agencies to fill open positions. Paper requisitions were still the norm, and often times, requisitions were not completed until after hires had already been made. In addition, reporting data were incomplete, making it difficult to deliver consistent measurements and process improvements.

After determining which areas needed the most attention, RES and Kellogg Company moved on to the next stage of the process.

Step Two: STRATEGIZE

Kellogg Company used the assessment to identify the following deliverables for RES:

- Integrated recruiting technology

- Recruiting specialists with highly developed competencies

- Improved overall function effectiveness, as measured by key metrics

- Reduction in overall costs

In deciding to outsource, Kellogg Company also began to question whether traditional recruiting roles were still relevant in their organization. For example, it was clear that RES would make use of the power of the Internet in its solution, but the skills of an Internet sourcer, or "Cybrarian," are very different from those of a traditional recruiter. Recruiters need to be marketing-oriented and free to focus on candidates at the candidates' convenience. As a result, Kellogg decided to introduce "relationship managers" as part of the recruiting team; these individuals would focus primarily on training and working with the hiring managers. "We needed to rethink traditional roles," Kilduff said. "One of the big advantages of outsourcing is the flexibility, the agility to respond to an organization's variable hiring needs." This ability, plus technology that was already in place at RES, laid the foundation for the outsourcing plan.

RES, in conjunction with Bernard Hodes Group, offered numerous advantages to Kellogg Company in its development of a more holistic approach to managing the staffing function. These advantages included:

- An Internet-based applicant management system that automated a broad range of recruitment activities (The RES proprietary system is called ROAM.)

- An integrated system to interact with Kellogg Company's own technology for employee referral and internal application processes

- Development of a "Careers" area on Kellogg.com

- On-site support staff to interact with hiring managers and with Human Resources staff

- An employment branding campaign

- All recruitment-related activities, from posting ads, sourcing resumes on the Internet, and networking to candidate screening and hiring manager contact

- Improvement of administrative processes, such as applicant tracking, report generation, and other activities

- Creative services for all recruitment marketing efforts.

Step Three: IMPLEMENT

Kellogg decided to implement all of the capabilities listed previously as a part of the outsourcing solution that RES would implement. RES and Kellogg Company took a number of steps to ensure a smooth transition to the new system. These included:

- Providing information about the new system to the various end-users in several formats (intranet, printed materials)

- Soliciting feedback from these users and acting on their feedback quickly

- Using internal champions to promote the benefits of outsourcing.

Training was also a key component of the implementation process. Initially, RES conducted training in group sessions at Kellogg Company facilities. However, it quickly became apparent that managers who did not have current hiring needs would not make learning about the new system a priority. To address this situation, RES developed a "just-in-time" training package that went to each manager as a new hiring request was made. (See more information under "Continuous Improvement" on the next page.)

The installation phase of the implementation effort was planned to run approximately three months. This time frame proved to be too ambitious, however. Although many of the planned communication pieces (such as a

"Staffing Gazette" informational Web-site, brochures, virtual postcards, promotional items and a training video) were ready to go on time, software development was not completed and management support was not fully in position, when the launch date arrived. It is to address such situations that the Hodes 360 process has, inherent within each of its steps, the capability for continuous improvement.

CONTINUOUS IMPROVEMENT ("Tweaking")

Initially, some of Kellogg Company's hiring managers questioned the "prudence" of the new approach. They were accustomed to using outside recruiting agencies and following their own processes. In addition, the original implementation timetable proved unrealistic, once the full scope of the requirements was uncovered. As more was learned, more technology customization and enhancements were required, all of which took longer than originally planned.

And, there were other problems. Despite well-intentioned efforts across the board, the expectations of hiring managers were not being met and hiring goals were not being reached. Nevertheless, Kellogg Company and RES were determined to make the partnership work. They developed an action plan that focused as much on the human side of problem-solving as on the technology of the solution. Placing the on-site staff under a microscope, it became obvious that the original recruiting team had to be upgraded, and in a couple of instances, team members had to be replaced. RES made the necessary changes and additions. Kellogg took additional steps. Even though recruiting activities had been outsourced, Cyd Kilduff decided that internal acceptance of the program would require a stronger joint effort that acknowledged and addressed user concerns. An internal champion, Andre Goodlett, was hired to oversee the project and to support it from the top down. His contributions quickly began to make a difference.

It also became clear that not all hiring managers were reviewing candidates submitted by RES in a timely manner. Kellogg Company and RES jointly reached out to the managers by implementing a one-on-one training program. This approach enabled each manager to get comfortable with the technology and with RES, without the pressure of being observed by an audience of their peers.

Once the managers were trained on the new system, a report was developed to ensure that candidates were being reviewed promptly. Whenever candidate information is not reviewed within five days of receipt, a "no review" report is automatically generated and sent to that hiring manager as well as to Andre Goodlett and the RES program managers. The report keeps the lines of communication open between candidates, hiring managers, HR and RES and ensures that top talent doesn't get "lost" while waiting for their credentials to be reviewed.

Although Kellogg Company recognizes the value of outside search firms in certain situations, the extensive use of such vendors also had to be addressed. RES and Kellogg Company worked together to formulate policies and develop a methodology that would integrate search firms into the new system. Kellogg Company notified all 80 search firms with which it had previously worked that they would have to operate within the framework of the RES ROAM system in order to remain eligible for future assignments. Under this framework, RES submits requirements information to the search firms, handles all communications with them, provides one-on-one training to them, and manages their relationship with Kellogg Company. The end result is that, in those rare instances where outside search is required, the Kellogg Company HR department is now able to track search firm activity and authorize payment within the same overall hiring management system. (Note: RES is primarily responsible for filling positions below the Director level. Kellogg Company continues its partnerships with many fine search firms who work on a variety of levels, but most particularly for positions at Director and above.)

Today, recruiters continue to train as needed, while building solid relationships with hiring managers. Changes continue to be made to the technology components of the system as new ideas and better methods emerge. Relationships have become stronger with the support of management on both sides of the partnership. And, one-by-one, previously skeptical departments and managers have been won over by the system's success in fulfilling their hiring needs. In short, it is a long-term improvement process that works.

Step Four: MEASURE

By every measure, the selection of RES as an outsourcing provider has been a success for Kellogg Company. For example, at the beginning of implementation in 2000, RES was filling just 10% of the vacancies at Kellogg; in October of 2001, it was filling 95% of those openings. During the same period, time-to-hire went from 67 days to just 39 days. By February of 2003, it fell further, to an average of 26 days. And perhaps most impressively, cost-per-hire has been reduced by over 64%.

In the Kellogg system, performance is tracked with a series of reports (25 different reports are available online, in real time), and by conducting regular customer satisfaction surveys with hiring managers. Satisfaction is measured for both the process and the RES staff, using such metrics as the level of service provided and the quality of candidates submitted. The scale is 1-5, with 5 being the highest. Results are determined for each requisition, so individual recruiters are reviewed, as well, to assess their level of performance. Satisfaction is high, with scores typically in the 4.25 – 4.75 range.

<u>LESSONS LEARNED</u>

As this case study clearly illustrates, any successful outsourcing process takes time, a lot of cooperation, and, most importantly, constant communication between all of the parties involved. RES and Kellogg Company are still working on continuous process improvements, but if they had to do it over again, they would make the following adjustments:

1) If you intend to reduce headcount as a result of outsourcing, limit your reductions until the outsourcing capability is in position and functioning at the basic levels;

2) Be as flexible and generous as possible in establishing a time frame for rollout, training, technology customization, and overall implementation of the program;

3) Identify a Project Manager for in-house implementation at the <u>inception</u> of the process and assign them two primary responsibilities: serving as liaison with the outsourcing partner and acting as an advocate for the program;

4) Identify key internal customers, and focus a "pilot" program on their needs. This approach enables you to do your "tweaking" before introducing the system to the company as a whole. It will also create internal champions in those areas that need the most help from the outsourcing partner.

THE FUTURE

Now that the Kellogg Company/RES outsourcing program has become an established success, what's next? Kilduff says,

> "We want to get to the point where we're measuring results rather than just efficiency. How

do we ensure delivery of value-added services? How can we make sure we are getting the best qualified candidates, who stay with us? We want to improve retention, and in our next phase of working together, we plan to develop an online tool to measure quality over our new hires' first year."

To accomplish these goals, RES plans to work more closely with Kellogg's hiring managers as they develop selection criteria for their openings. A system of follow-ups throughout a new hire's first year on-the-job will then illustrate how well they are meeting these criteria.

In addition, performance as measured against the most important goals of the outsourcing program – Efficiency (Cost reduction), Speed, Satisfaction, and Quality – is continually being improved. From Kilduff's perspective, the biggest benefits of outsourcing for Kellogg Company are: the ability of an experienced vendor to introduce new technology quickly; and its own ability to bring more resources to bear on a variety of different issues, and integrate them effectively through the outsourcing vendor. "Most importantly, we need agility to respond quickly, effectively, and nimbly to shifting needs," she says. "Every part of our business must be able to respond quickly to change! RES, as an outsourcing partner, has truly given us the agility to address a huge variety of hiring needs."

Chapter 3

Key Set #3
It's All in the Marketing Mix

The recruiting and staffing process is both an art and a science. As a consequence, there are numerous variables that can impact a company's hiring and retention programs. From a scientific perspective, current methodologies must be reviewed, changes need to be recommended, and best practices put into action before a company can truly become a world-class recruiting and staffing organization. But from an artistic perspective, there are also many intangible factors, such as taste, timing and chemistry, that play a huge role in determining a staffing function's level of success.

It is not a coincidence that these two perspectives exist within the recruiting and staffing function. Back in 1970, Bernard S. Hodes opened a recruitment advertising agency with a revolutionary approach to servicing clients. Mr. Hodes believed that recruiting was a *marketing* activity—both an art and a science—rather than a process within personnel administration. It's taken over 30 years to happen, but today, very few HR executives would dispute that modern staffing organizations must, indeed, apply the principles and practices of effective marketing in order to survive, much less prevail in the War for Talent.

The primary components of marketing are planning, pricing, promotion, and distribution. The degree of staffing success or failure is "all in the mix" — the delicate blending of these components into the recipe that is right for your particular situation. Moreover, the same practices that a company uses to market its products and/or services can also be applied to the recruiting and staffing function. There's no single "magic bullet" when it comes to recruitment marketing; instead, creativity across all of the components is what counts. Let's start by looking at the first component of a successful marketing mix: effective planning.

A. PLANNING

Any strong marketing endeavor begins with a solid plan, based on projections for the future. According to the Bureau of National Affairs (BNA), median employee separation rates (excluding layoffs, reductions in staff and departures of temporary staff) averaged 1.1% of employers' workforces per month for 2001, down from 1.3% for 2000.[10] A conservative conclusion, therefore, is that a 10% annual attrition rate is the best an average company can anticipate achieving. Given the Bureau of Labor Statistics projections for manpower shortages that I discussed in Chapter 1, however, this turnover ratio is bound to increase.

Such projections may come as a surprise to many in light of the current surplus of workers. But, this labor shortage is actually minor when compared to the SKILLS shortage that experts are predicting for the future. Such high skill occupations as programmers and electronic engineers, for example, will soon be in very short supply. Other occupations, such as nurses and truck drivers, are already experiencing severe shortages. Smart organizations—those that will survive and thrive under these conditions—are taking steps not only to retain their skilled employees, but to activate a plan that will continue to attract them.

This preparation is best achieved if an organization has written goals and strategies that are periodically adjusted for changes in the recruitment marketplace. How many times have you observed or worked for a company where things are done a certain way because "that's how we've always done it?" With goals and a plan to achieve them laid out in writing, it's much easier for employees to get on the same page and work with a common purpose. Without such planning for the future, on the other hand, it's easy to get mired in reactive recruiting – filling a job pipeline only after an opening exists. The push to fill an open position, and fill it fast, takes over the staffing department's focus and time. As a consequence, they cannot proactively search for and may miss out on top talent, simply because they are captive of the requirements of the moment. Yet, well managed organizations—those that have a plan for the future—know that there will always be a place for good candidates.

Planning begins by either doing a self-assessment, or bringing in a third party to assist with such an evaluation. The simplest assessment consists of asking yourself the following four questions:

1) How much are you currently spending on all recruiting and staffing activities?

2) How will you adjust these expenditures to align with your future hiring requirements?

3) How are you measuring results?

4) Do you think you can do better, and, if so, how much better?

It's likely that the answers to these four questions will encourage you to do a more in-depth assessment of your staffing function. For example, you may want to take a look at:

- Goal setting

- Benchmark studies for Best Practices

- Recruitment and staffing process mapping

- Response management analysis

- Candidate tracking analysis

- Sourcing analysis

- Screening and selection criteria evaluation

- Satisfaction studies of both hiring managers and candidates

- Corporate and career Web-site content and usage analysis

- Internal focus group studies

- Internal and external perception of employment brand studies

- Media habits surveys

You might even want to go further and do a "stretch" assessment that would include in-depth evaluations of the following staffing activities:

1. **Requisition Management:** How many and what categories of requisitions are open now? How many requisitions have been filled within the last 12 months? How many of each category do you anticipate over the next 12 months?

2. **Commitment to Talent:** How committed is top management to winning the War for Talent? How

committed is your organization not only to recruiting the best, but to keeping and upgrading existing talent?

3. **Position as an Employer:** Why do people join your company? Why do they leave? Why do they stay? Who's your competition? How do candidates view you as a potential employer? What could your company be doing better?

4. **Culture:** How would you define your organization's culture? Is that definition what you'd like it to be? Are you aligning all staffing activities with the culture you seek to achieve?

5. **Hiring Process:** What are your organization's plans and strategies for making the best hires in the shortest time, at the lowest cost? Who are the players in, and what are the components of, your hiring process? What level of satisfaction does this process produce among hiring managers as well as candidates?

6. **Technology:** Are you equipped with automated systems that combine state-of-the-art functionality with user friendliness? What are your expectations of technology – are you avoiding it, do you expect

technology, alone, to do the vast majority of the work or do you have a more balanced view?

7. **Marketing Promotions:** What's your employment branding strategy? (If you have one!) Does it align with the company's overall product/services marketing message? Do you have a state-of-the-art career Web-site? What print, interactive and/or electronic advertising techniques do you use? How well are these various elements working, and how consistent are your messages? Do you maintain a proactive campaign or just a reactive one? Do you have an active public relations effort dedicated to staffing?

8. **Metrics:** What do you measure? How accurate are your measurements? What would you like to measure? How do you stack up against the competition when it comes to cost, speed, candidate and new hire quality, and candidate and hiring manager satisfaction with your recruiting efforts?

Upon completion of your audit, you will have a report card that identifies where you stand and what your organization needs to improve. Most likely, you'll conclude that you have a great deal of work to do. If that's the case, put your goals and methodologies for improvement in writing so that they can serve as the basis for your overall plan.

Before you begin, however, you've got to have measures in place to be sure that your improvements are actually working. The best way to do so is to establish "trackable" metrics in such individual areas as candidate and new hire quality, candidate and hiring manager satisfaction, time, and cost or, collectively, your return on investment (ROI). What really matters here is that you set up consistent metrics with consistent definitions for measuring your own performance from one time period to another, rather than measuring your organization's performance against other organizations that may or may not use metrics and definitions that are identical to yours.

The measurements that I suggest you use include:

1. **QUALITY:** What is the quality of the hires being made? How long do they stay with the company?

Is there excessive turnover in a certain area, and if so, why?

2. **SATISFACTION:** What is the satisfaction level of the various parties involved in the recruitment process? (This measurement should cover hiring managers, candidates, and human resources staff.) How are you currently tracking customer satisfaction with the recruitment process? (Are you tracking it at all?) What practices could be improved? Is there a more efficient way to manage administrative functions? Do you treat both hiring managers and candidates as if they were customers?

3. **TIME:** What is the average time-to-hire? How can it be improved upon? What factors are contributing to a lengthy time-to-hire? Can time-to-hire be tracked for various departments/job categories within the organization?

4. **COST:** Here, I recommend that you use a formula developed by an organization called Staffing.org. It measures recruiting and staffing costs (internal as well as external) as a percentage of total first year compensation paid to individuals recruited.

According to Staffing.org studies over 3 years, the average staffing efficiency ratio is 13.8% (not including relocation).[11] Since it is very likely that those participating in the study were well above average (or they would not have participated), any organization with a staffing efficiency at or below 13.8% deserves high marks. However, the cost of recruiting is a much less revealing measure than such metrics as the contribution per employee (total revenue ÷ total employees), the cost of jobs remaining vacant, and the cost of mediocre hires. These factors are discussed in further detail in Chapter 4.

When you are able to measure candidate and new hire quality, candidate and hiring manager satisfaction, time, and costs as they relate to recruitment and staffing, you can establish reliable benchmarks for planning a sound recruiting strategy for the future. For a more detailed discussion of metrics, please see the Afterword.

B.   PRICING (Total Employee Remuneration)

The second component of a sound mix of recruitment practices involves how your organization remunerates its employees. Compensation is a major factor within the "pricing" component. However, when I say " compensation," I'm including more than just salary. In my view, compensation also encompasses such elements as incentive pay and bonuses, medical benefits, savings plans, workplace flexibility, time-off policies, and more. You can have a stellar plan for attracting top-notch talent, but without a competitive and creative incentive package, that talent is likely to look elsewhere. Attracting great candidates means that you've got to have some flexibility when it comes to compensating them. In order to attract and retain the best possible employees, companies must be aware of what compensation packages are being offered by the competition, and strive to be equal or better.

<u>Unique Selling Propositions</u>

Fortunately, for many companies, compensation is just one component of the "mix" candidates are looking for when they accept a new position. They are also seeking intangibles related to job satisfaction. In fact, David Maister, noted author and lecturer, has compiled the following list of what he refers to as "non-financial incentives:"[12]

- approval

- gratitude

- autonomy

- participation/involvement

- personal interest/support

- public recognition

- visibility (inside and outside the office)

- contacts

- access to information ("being an insider")

- access to additional resources

- rapid response (access to the manager)

- task support

- titles (official and unofficial)

- special roles or assignments

- challenge

- meaning

As part of your recruitment planning strategy, your company will need to identify its unique selling propositions: What makes your organization a great place to work? It could be the casual atmosphere, where titles mean little and teamwork is emphasized. It could be your company's history – the first in its field to offer a particular product or service. Or, it could be directly related to your company's products and services (e.g., an athletic apparel company that sponsors the Special Olympics, a bank that offers free financial services to its employees, or a retailer that provides a big employee discount on its products). People are drawn to organizations that support something they believe in, or that can provide something that's attractive to them.

Creative Workplace Incentives

The packaging of creative workplace incentives can be one of the factors that makes your organization a unique place to work and, as a result, tip the scale in its favor. Workplace flexibility, for example, can be very attractive to potential employees, now that it's possible to work from practically anywhere. If your company is willing to let a terrific candidate work from home a few days a week, or job-share, or work non-traditional hours, that willingness to "think outside the box" can be a huge differentiating factor. So too can such arrangements as additional vacation time, unpaid leave of absence, or a 4-day workweek. The possibilities are endless, and can go a long way toward making your organization attractive, even if your competition offers higher salaries.

C. PROMOTION (Marketing Promotions)

As I mentioned earlier, there is no single "magic bullet" that is guaranteed to work when it comes to promotional activities. However there is one "magic ingredient" that can turn each bullet from lead to silver. That ingredient is CREATIVITY, and its power should never be underestimated. An organization's ability to express its unique recruiting proposition cleverly and consistently represents a truly awesome competitive edge.

There are as many ways to promote a company as there are candidates to reach. When I started my career in recruitment advertising, there were few options available – classified ads in newspapers and trade publications, and (for the daring) radio commercials. Today, the options are virtually limitless, and as a consequence, creative promotional activities are a precondition for attracting top talent. Some of the venues with which you can market your job opportunities include:

Newspapers	Job Postings on Job Boards
Magazines	Banners on Niche Sites
Newsletters	Chat Groups
Organizations	Online Communities
Broadcast Radio & Television	Webcast
Outdoor/Transit	Banners on Portals
Direct Mail	Email and Virtual Postcards
Recruiting Events	Virtual Events
Search/Employment Agencies	Research/Resume Mining
Direct Recruiting	Data Pods and Push Technology

However, regardless of the promotional activities you choose, any marketing campaign should start with a branding strategy that drives all candidate traffic to a user-friendly career Web-site, that includes an up-to-date and easily searchable jobs database. This effort can include proactive, generic (meaning non job-specific) messages in newspapers, trade publications, consumer magazines, online banners, broadcast radio and television, employee referral programs, movie screens, bumper stickers, hot air balloons ... whatever will reach your audience. Then, you can supplement those efforts with reactive (or job-specific) listings on job boards, your online employee referral program, your internal mobility site, and in newspapers, trade publications, and at other appropriate places.

The right mix is best determined by measuring results. And the most accurate, most consistent way to gather data that will identify which promotional efforts work best is to funnel all responses through a single gateway: your company's career Web-site. The Web-site bridges the gap between marketing promotions and technology. This connection brings us to the next component of the mix, Distribution.

D. DISTRIBUTION (Hiring Management Process)

In product marketing, the activities of planning, pricing and promotions are a total waste of money if the distribution process fails to enable the consumer to make a purchase easily while at the store, on a Web-site, or the telephone. When it comes to recruiting and staffing, the hiring management process represents distribution, and the hire represents the purchase. Requisitions have to be completed and approved through various channels. Candidates have to enter the hiring process and be matched with a specific position (or area of interest). Hiring managers have to be able to review candidate information and share it with other decision-makers. These are just a few of the ways that information must be distributed within an organization's hiring management system. And, to be most effective, it should all be done on the Internet, in real-time.

What's the best way to achieve a seamless hiring management (distribution) process? You'll need to implement a number of components that combine state-of-the-art technology with good, old fashioned recruiting. These include:

1. **Requisition Database:** This resource should be the first stop when a hiring manager has an opening. Ideally, a requisition database is shared by the entire company. It should contain standardized job descriptions that can be customized for the needs of specific departments and/or regions. It should have a clearly outlined approval process, facilitated by e-mail. It should feed into a job posting system. As candidates apply for a position, reports can be pulled by its requisition number. Measurements of the number and source of candidates, cost-per-hire and time-to-hire should also be accessible by requisition number. As you can see, a robust, well-maintained requisition database is likely to revolutionize the efficiency of your staffing department.

2. **Job Posting System:** The requisition database feeds the job posting system, thereby eliminating duplication of effort. The job posting goes, first, to a company's internal job posting system; then, to

the company's career Web-site; and finally, out to external job boards and other media, as necessary.

3. **Online Response Management:** Once the job is posted, candidates should be able to apply and receive confirmation that their resume has been received and updates on their status online. Candidates from every source as well as those who aren't applying for a specific job can be referred to an online response form. Such online response forms also can be used with other recruitment activities, such as your employee referral and internal mobility programs.

4. **Candidate Management/Tracking:** Candidates should be assigned status codes throughout the review process, so that hiring managers and HR can get real-time status updates at a glance. The system should also allow for the entry of comments by those involved in candidate evaluation. The system can then be programmed with prompts to take whatever action is appropriate, whether it's to review resumes, schedule an interview, or complete paperwork. In

this way, candidates won't get lost during the hiring process.

5. **Relationship Marketing:** Probably the best, long-term tool for companies trying to attract top talent is relationship marketing. And relationship marketing can now be extraordinarily efficient with an Internet-based recruitment process.

It all begins with your candidate database, but that database is useful only if it's full of recent, searchable candidate information. Let's say Susan Smith has applied for a position as a Senior Programmer at your company. She doesn't have enough work experience for the position, but her educational credentials are strong. Since she applied online and you have her email address, the system is able to notify her automatically. The message informs her that she didn't qualify for the opening for which she applied, but that there may be other openings in the future that are a match. It then asks if she would be interested in learning about these opportunities when they arise. Susan responds in the affirmative, and a few months go by. During this period, the automated system has sent her regular updates on your company's redesigned Web-site, links to articles in her area of interest, and other related information. Then, a job opens up that's a good fit with Susan. Since a dialogue has been opened between her and your company, the odds are in your favor that she'll be interested in your new opportunity. In the process, everyone wins – Susan gets the job, and your company has made good use of its existing candidate data, without incurring additional recruiting expenses.

6. **Employee Referral Program:** An employee referral program (EmRP) should be designed to assist a company in its recruiting efforts by enlisting the help of employees in referring candidates who might be a strong fit for open positions. Instead of paying large sums of money to search firms, employers encourage employees to refer friends and associates and pay bonuses or prizes to the employee if their referrals are hired. An online EmRP typically consists of a Web-site housing an online referral form, general

information about the program, its rules and regulations, Frequently Asked Questions (FAQs), and a list of open positions. Acknowledgement e-mails (or letters) should be forwarded to the appropriate employees and individual referrals whenever a referral is first made. Then, every time there is a change in the candidate's status, the employee should be sent an update via e-mail. As a cost-effective recruiting tool, it's hard to beat an EmRP.

7. **Internal Mobility System (IMS):** The IMS is an automated tool that allows your company to post open positions internally. Employees access the IMS to apply for openings within the company. Such a system typically consists of an employee site that lists openings and directions on how to apply for them, and a hiring manager site that allows them to manage requisitions and communicate privately with employees.

8. **Hiring Process Workflow:** The best recruitment marketing and recruiting efforts will fail if a user-friendly, streamlined hiring process is not conceived, implemented and maintained to everyone's satisfaction. All of the tools and

processes previously listed are components of a strong, Internet-based hiring process workflow. (Further details appear on page 144.)

9. **Metrics and Reports:** To be effective, each of these distribution tools must be measurable. You can evaluate what's working and what's not, and make adjustments based on REAL, fully-reported data. Technology enables reports to be available at the touch of a few keys, and lets members of an organization share data easily.

A Winning Formula

Successful companies know that it takes an across-the-board effort to attract and keep good employees. It's never just one thing, but rather a combination of many factors that sets apart employers of choice. With insightful planning, creative workplace incentive packages, innovative promotions, and a cutting-edge hiring management system to tie them all together, you can create the right marketing mix and build a world-class recruiting and staffing organization.

Chapter 4

Key Set #4
Flexibility and Hiring for a Culture Fit

So far, you've made a number of changes to work towards becoming an employer of choice; you've improved your efforts in the cycle of response and responsiveness; and you've strengthened your mix of recruitment tools to attract top-flight candidates. Now that you've met the challenges of attracting strong potential employees, you'll want to be sure that you hire and KEEP the right person for each job and for the company as a whole.

I can't emphasize enough how important it is for the long-term growth of your organization to hire for the tightest possible culture fit. Bad hires—those where the employee-culture fit is uncomfortable—are very expensive!

Consider these figures: In the Staffing.org survey mentioned in Chapter 3, the cost of recruiting over the last three years averages 13.8% of a new hire's first year compensation. That sounds like a lot until you consider the cost of making a hiring mistake. Bliss & Associates, a management consulting firm, claims that turnover costs a company at least 150% of the previous incumbent's compensation package, and the percentage increases to 200-250% for sales people and managers.[13] Moreover, many believe these figures are much too conservative. Dr. John Sullivan points to the fact that selecting the wrong software engineer can cost a company a million dollars, and the wrong CEO can cost in excess of one billion. As Dr. Sullivan notes, "Great hires make us rich … mediocre hires cost us a bundle."[14]

Given the very real challenge involved in becoming an employer of choice, no company can afford the heavy losses caused by mediocre hires, attrition and vacancies. Just look at the consequences of what I call the "Vicious Cycle of Mediocre Hires."

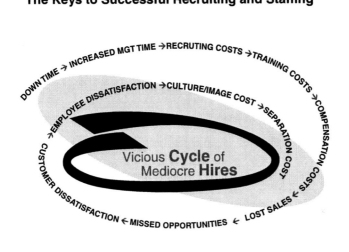

Think about it: When a job is vacant, you have the downtime to account for and the increased management time incurred by "filling in." Then, you have recruiting costs for the replacement, followed immediately by training costs to get the new person ready for their responsibilities. Later, of course, you also have the compensation costs of the new employee. And if this new employee isn't up-to-speed at first, or worse, never gets up-to-speed, what about the missed opportunities? Lost sales? The costs of dissatisfaction among customers as well as other employees? And what about the impact on your culture and image? Then, if you decide you must replace the person, you have separation costs, and the cycle begins all over again with downtime and so on. However you want to calculate these costs, there can be no doubt that they are huge.

The key to avoiding this cycle is the fourth and final key to successful recruiting, "Flexibility and Hiring for a Culture Fit."

FLEXIBILITY

Norm Snell, director of global compensation and benefits for Cisco Systems, says that a company "can only tinker with compensation and benefits systems so much; it's culture, culture, culture that must drive staffing and retention systems."[15] That said, "tinkering" with other factors in the hiring process CAN make a difference between hiring and retaining the best people and unnecessarily losing talent as a result of inflexible recruiting and staffing processes.

For example, forcing recruiters to adhere to a rigid set of criteria in filling an opening will only produce someone who has done a specific job at a specific company. That set of attributes will not necessarily be indicative of how productive this individual will be within YOUR organization and culture. Hence, it's important to be flexible enough to accept trade-offs; or to put it another way, hire for culture fit, not necessarily for exact job fit. This flexibility enables you both to attract and keep productive employees.

To illustrate how flexibility in the hiring process can make a significant impact on your organization's core culture, it's important to look at the following five areas:

- job descriptions and requirements

  (what employees do),

- the interview and offer process,

- work schedules (when employees work),

- work locations (where employees work), and

- compensation packages.

1. JOB DESCRIPTIONS & REQUIREMENTS

Flexibility in job specifications is often a sore point between hiring managers and recruiters. The "perfect candidate" may never get the hiring manager's attention because they lack a specified area of study, degree, or years of experience. Since we are already facing a shortage of skills, a shortage that is destined to grow exponentially, it's important for employers not to get hung up on impossible and/or nonessential job requirements. In fact, job specifications need to be written to allow for trade-offs. Be willing to waive the specific degree if the candidate has the right experience. Accept five years' experience and the perfect attitude in place of the 10 years' experience that you want.

2. THE INTERVIEW AND OFFER PROCESS

Now, more than ever, hiring managers and Human Resource professionals need to make themselves available at the candidate's convenience, not the other way around. If you truly intend to make recruiting and staffing a marketing function, you'll treat applicants as customers. Making the effort to interview during lunch hours, after work, or even on weekends will go a long way toward showing that your organization is committed to doing whatever it takes to accommodate top candidates.

In today's competitive market for top talent, it's extremely important to MAKE THE OFFER when you (or the hiring manager) have seen an ideal applicant. Don't make them come back for numerous interviews; take action before someone else does, or you'll miss out on a great hire. In addition, encourage hiring managers to employ appropriate talent who fit your culture and worry about their acquiring specific job skills later. Help hiring managers understand that they can no longer ask to see 5 more "ideal" candidates, after interviewing a top prospect. The depth of talent to sustain such an endless process no longer exists.

3. WORK SCHEDULES

According to research conducted by Wharton School of Business Professor Stewart Friedman (and others), when employers give more scheduling freedom to employees – regardless of how many hours the employees must work – the result is greater productivity and increased morale. The data backs this view up: at Johnson &

Johnson, workers on flextime schedules averaged 50% less absenteeism than those on fixed schedules. At a Xerox customer service center, when managers turned over scheduling to the employees, they saw a 30% reduction in absenteeism.[16] In other words, think twice before turning down an applicant simply because they cannot or will not work the "normal" or traditional schedule in your organization.

In addition to offering flextime and/or a compressed work week you might also consider job sharing as an employee benefit. According to a 1999 Society for Human Resource Management (SHRM) survey, 22% of U.S. companies were offering some type of job sharing. Among larger companies (with more than 5,000 workers), a surprising 59% let employees share jobs, said Kristen Accipiter, a spokesperson for SHRM.

"Scheduling flexibility is the single greatest non-financial tool at your disposal for winning battles in the talent wars," says Bruce Tulgan, internationally recognized as the leading expert on young people in the workplace.[17] To recruit and/or retain the best people, it's worth the effort to customize a schedule to their needs. More and more companies are realizing that offering flextime, telecommuting, and part-time work schedules is a smart way to attract and retain their top performers. Everyone wins: employees are more invested in their work, since they are able to create a schedule around their needs; and employers don't have to spend time and money attempting to replace valuable talent.

4. WORK LOCATIONS

The most recent U.S. Department of Labor study (released in March, 1998) reports that there were 23.3 million people who did some of their work from home in 1997. A more recent survey by Telework America projects that there may be as many as 30 million regular "teleworkers" by the end of 2004.

In short, telecommuting is definitely here to stay. When workers are given the opportunity to work from home, it's been shown to increase productivity, provide higher job satisfaction, lower overhead costs, and improve retention rates. And yet, many companies are slow to offer this option to qualified applicants and/or their employees. According to the study "Nothing But Net," 41% of workers said that with proper technology, they could do their jobs from a remote location. They also reported that only 16% of their employers offered them such an option.[18] Workers want and expect more control, and they are looking for ways to strike a balance between their busy home and work lives. With logistical concerns about telecommuting becoming less of an issue, we can anticipate an explosion in this form of work in the near future.

5. COMPENSATION PACKAGES

Top talent is worth paying more to get and to keep, period. Dr. John Sullivan recently presented an interesting case for why top performers are worth the extra compensation. His analysis showed that top performers rarely earn over 40% more than what average workers earn for the same job. In contrast, organizations that have estimated the performance (or contribution) differential between average and top performing employees have found that it is often 300% higher![19]

Compensation is the one investment for hiring and keeping top performers where you are sure to gain a significant return. To become an employer of choice, therefore, your efforts should be focused on bringing in and rewarding top performers – you can't afford not to.

Of course, there are many ways to compensate employees that are non-financial. For example, I included David Maister's list of "non-financial currencies" in Chapter 3.

It's interesting to compare what employees value most in a workplace and what supervisors THINK their employees value. Number one on the list of important job elements for employees is "appreciation for good work," yet that ranks eighth on the supervisor's list. Number two for employees is "feeling 'in' on things," and that ranks dead last (out of ten) from the supervisor's perspective! Traditionally, managers rank salary and job security as the most important job conditions, while employees put these factors in the middle.[20]

Bruce Tulgan claims there are five non-financial factors in an employment relationship about which people care the most:[21]

1. When they work (schedule)

2. Where they work (location)

3. What they do (tasks and responsibilities)

4. Who they work with

5. What they are (or are not) learning on the job

Sadly, most companies continue to overlook intangible forms of compensation and benefits, whether it is flexibility in work hours and location or simply a culture that fosters a sense of appreciation for workers' efforts. Employers of choice recognize that it's the combination of ALL of these factors that makes up the core culture of the organization. And workplace culture spells the difference between organizations that thrive – consistently recruiting and retaining top talent – and those that merely survive.

BEST RECRUITMENT CULTURES

What is "culture?"

In the world of business, culture has been described as "deep seated traditions and widely accepted and shared beliefs that govern business organizations just like they did primitive tribes."[22] Or, as stated by Marvin Bower, long time McKinsey & Company managing director, "the way we do things around here." A strong culture is a system of informal rules that spells out how people are to behave most of the time.

Workplace culture drives how everything within an organization is done, from the top down. It is the secret to successful selection, retention, and reward systems, and is such a critical component of hiring that it's cited as the number one reason for turnover. "A strong culture enables people to feel better about what they do, so they are more likely to work harder." says Terrence Deal and Allan Kennedy in their book *Corporate Cultures*.[23] Employers of choice understand that they have a responsibility to create and maintain a strong culture that connects with their employees.

The elements of workplace culture include:

- The business environment
- Company values
- Heroes in the organization
- Rites and rituals and
- The cultural network within the company.

Companies with a strong culture clearly define their values and beliefs and emphasize specific priorities. Every area of the company shares these fundamental beliefs, expressing them with organized and consistent practices and rituals. The focus of the company is outward and long-term. Morale is high.

Defining a company's culture requires more than simply observing employee behavior. The physical setting of the company is important, as is the literature it produces. For example, see how the company greets strangers and observe how people spend their time. What are the career path progressions? How long do people stay in their jobs? What are some of the anecdotes passing through the informal company network? Does the company have an articulated set of beliefs, and do people in the organization know what they are?

Today's companies know that people are their real competitive advantage and that attracting and retaining the right people is crucial to their future success. Their goal, therefore, is to find new employees who support the company's core culture, and keep the ones who already do. When the company articulates a strong cultural message, it becomes possible to hire people with a strong culture fit, rather than focusing on job fit alone. A good culture fit involves hiring people with similar skills, interests and values that align with those of the organization. In other words, " although job fit is important, culture fit determines whether someone is highly likely to remain with and be successful with the company."[24]

An outstanding book on this subject is *Finding and Keeping Great Employees*, by Jim Harris and Joan Brannick. They investigated Best Practices at a variety of organizations to determine how progressive companies leverage their core purpose and corporate culture to attract and retain top talent. They conclude that "Companies with world-class staffing and retention practices see their culture as vital to their organization; they understand culture as the basis for selecting and rewarding people."[25]

So, begin by defining your organization's core culture. Then, your objective should be to <u>align</u> all staffing and retention processes with that core culture in a strategic way. According to Bruce Tulgan, the best recruitment cultures provide:[26]

- Marketable skills
- Access to decision-makers

- Personal credit for results achieved

- Clear area of responsibility

- Chance for creative expression.

If you are looking to improve your recruiting and retention performance – and who isn't? – you'd be wise to weave these factors into your culture and make sure your efforts to do so are well publicized.

WORKPLACE CULTURE IN ACTION

Over the years, the two most prevalent common denominators that I've seen in client job specifications are a college degree and a certain number of years of experience working for a competitive organization. In hiring hundreds of employees over my 30+ year career with Bernard Hodes Group, I too have looked for a degree, preferably in marketing or advertising, and experience (ideally with our competitors or the media) in positions involving sales, service, management, creative, and/or presentation skills. Now, as I look back, I find myself coming to some surprising conclusions.

First of all, I would never have been able to get into the recruitment field had not Bob Dorskind and the late Eve Novak of Diener & Dorskind Advertising decided to overlook the standard job specifications. I really wasn't qualified, but they took a chance.

Second, Bernard S. Hodes and Marion Starr of Bernard Hodes Group refused to accept my resignation after my first three months with the organization. I had resigned because I felt I didn't fit the culture. They also made an exception in keeping me, because they focused on the intangibles and saw my fit with a new culture they wanted to install in the company.

Finally, the best hires I ever made weren't qualified (according to our job specs) ... and some of the worst hires I ever made certainly appeared to be qualified as they moved through the hiring process.

The vast majority of my best hires either came directly out of school, had no degree, and/or came with experience from organizations other than direct competitors or the media. How do I explain that? Since the culture at Bernard Hodes Group is the only common denominator, I believe it is the answer. Those who are most successful in our company are capable of making things happen on their own, with little supervision. The people who fit our culture best are dedicated to overcoming roadblocks and dealing with constant change, in their pursuit of solving client problems. Essentially, the people who've grown up through the Hodes ranks are innovative, resourceful, smart, creative entrepreneurs capable of wearing many hats. Anyone who's given an assignment and replies, "but, that's not my job," will not survive in this culture. They'll be driven out, not by their supervisors, but by their peers. And yet, despite such high expectations, our rate of attrition is very low compared to our competition.

To illustrate this idea further, I've selected the best hires I ever made and named them my "Magnificent Seven." Five of these talented individuals are still employed by Bernard Hodes Group. The other two made major contributions before moving on to tremendous success on their own. Take a look at their backgrounds:

Player 1: Came to us with a degree and six years' experience with a direct competitor, including work in sales, service, management and making presentations. This person was hired with the title of Branch Manager, progressed to Sr. Vice President and has been with us since 1983. Initially, I thought that this employee was the only member of the Magnificent Seven who met our standard job specifications prior to joining Bernard Hodes Group. However, I later learned that her degree was from a junior college, and we were looking for someone with a bachelor's degree. So, technically, this person did NOT meet our original specs.

Player 2: Came to us with no degree and a background in healthcare administration. She had absolutely no proven sales, management, or presentation skills. This person was hired with the title of Account Coordinator, progressed to Sr. Vice President and has performed effectively for us since 1985.

Player 3: Came to us with a degree in advertising and no experience of any kind. Once again, this person was hired with the title of Account Coordinator, progressed to Sr. Vice President and has done very well with us since 1988.

Player 4: Came to us with a degree and about two years of experience in Human Resources. He did have some service background, but little sales and no management or presentation skills. This person was hired as a Telephone Interviewer, progressed to Sr. Vice President and has been with us since 1986.

Player 5: Came to us with no degree and about five years of experience in the temporary staffing industry. There was no doubt that this person had service skills, but her management background was limited and her sales and presentation skills were untapped. We brought this person in as an Account Supervisor. She is now a Vice President and has been with us since 1998.

Player 6: Came to us at 19 years of age and with no degree. His background included limited creative and service skills, and no sales or presentation experience. We hired this person with the title of Designer. He progressed to Creative Director, and remained with us for over five years before going into his own successful video production business.

Player 7: Came to us with a degree and 6 months of experience writing low-end paperback novels in an assembly line environment. He had no sales, service, management, or presentation experience. We brought this person into the company as an Account Coordinator. He progressed to the title of Account Supervisor, and remained with us for about four years. There was no doubt in my mind that this individual was destined for great success. Despite my practical advice to the contrary, however, he left for Hollywood to pursue a career in the entertainment industry. Today, he is a famous movie and television producer.

The individual members of my Magnificent Seven are very different from one another. Four are men and three are women. They come from different parts of the country and have different ethnic backgrounds. Their political beliefs range from far right to far left, with everything in between. The only common denominators, then, are that none of them were qualified to be hired according to the original job specs, and every one of them turned out to be an innovative, resourceful, smart, creative entrepreneur capable of wearing many hats. No less important, not one of them has ever said; "but, that's not my job." These people have not only thrived in our company culture; they helped create it. The more I think about them, the more convinced I am that you can't recruit such people by sourcing and interviewing in strict accordance with traditional job specifications.

Recently, I was delighted to pick up a copy of Lou Adler's *Hire With Your Head* and find out that my Magnificent Seven revelation was far from unique. According to Lou: "Job descriptions must be redefined to reflect what needs to get done rather than what a candidate needs to have." [27] After studying hundreds, if not thousands of examples, he has concluded that over 90% of all hiring managers make poor hiring decisions. He is also convinced that "the best work harder than everyone else. They make an impact. They make things happen. They do more than required. They consistently deliver more results than expected, and they do it on time all the time." [28] In short, Lou's "Magnificent Thousands" very closely resemble my Magnificent Seven.

So how can you find your "Magnificent Ones?" Lou suggests a performance-based interviewing approach that treats outside candidates in a fashion identical to existing employees being considered for internal transfers. He says: "Traditional job descriptions listing skills, experience, academics, and competencies are misleading, can often preclude you from hiring top people, and should largely be ignored in the hiring process. In their place, profiles describing superior performance will be used." [29] Even with better sourcing and interviewing techniques, however, hiring mistakes will continue to be made. (After all, some people interview and test better than they perform.) An improved process, on the other hand, will limit the errors, and enable you to correct the mistakes when they are made.

That being said, we should all ask ourselves: Would we have the vision and courage to hire someone like Bill Porter? Bill was born with cerebral palsy, and was told for many years that he was unemployable. In other words, he could not meet any employer's traditional job specifications. Finally, the Watkins Company took a chance on him, and for the next 40+ years, he walked eight to ten miles a day, often in extreme difficulty and pain, and became the company's top door-to-door salesman. In the process, he's probably contributed more to the Watkins brand and bottom line than any other employee in the company. His story has been told by 20/20, a *Reader's Digest* feature entitled "Ten Things I

Learned from Bill Porter," and a TNT movie called "Door to Door." At 69, Bill is still going strong. I urge you to learn more about Bill at www.billporter.com.

ASSESSMENT TOOLS FOR THE HIRING PROCESS

Almost every organization uses the same basic hiring process (see the "Cycle of Response and Responsiveness" in Chapter 2). It begins with defining the job, and then moves on to evaluating applicants, making a decision on whom to hire, and evaluating/measuring the results. A recent survey by Global Learning Resources, Inc., shows that in addition to these basic screening steps, 75% of all organizations use some type of competency analyses as criteria for assessing candidates for key positions.[30]

These assessment tools range from simple telephone screening to more in-depth selection tools, which are now in surprisingly widespread use. Of the latter, those that relate to hiring for a culture fit include personality tests, "fit" tests, situational judgment tests, and simulations. A brief summary of the pros and cons of each of these instruments follows.

A) **Personality tests:** Probably the most common selection tool, personality tests are useful in determining if an individual is likely to fit in well with the existing corporate culture. They are usually a good predictor of future performance, but can be perceived as "too personal" by applicants, especially when they ask questions that are not clearly job-related.

B) **"Fit" tests:** These tests attempt to match people with organizations and jobs based on values. "Fit" tests are likely to grow in popularity as they provide data on what employees value in a work environment that can be helpful in developing retention strategies. However, it's difficult to measure "fit" since it's based on factors that vary from organization to organization.

C) **Situational judgment tests:** Applicants are placed in a work-related situation, and evaluated based on their reactions to certain cues. Situational judgment tests are very effective predictors of job performance, especially in evaluating such competencies as interpersonal skills, business acumen, and decision-making abilities.[31] Of course, the drawback with these tests is that the behavior of the applicant during the test may be very different from their behavior when they are faced with a similar situation on-the-job.

D) **Simulations:** Well designed simulations are highly job-related and evaluate all of the key aspects of on-the-job performance. If simulations were less expensive and time-consuming to administer, they would undoubtedly be at the top of the list of assessment practices. Besides being legally defensible, they are clearly among the most valid tools for predicting future success on-the-job. However, some people who do poorly on simulations, may still perform well when placed in an actual job environment.

While simulations may be the best predictor of on-the-job performance, you cannot give everyone who applies for a job a "tryout." The next best thing is to interview the candidate in such a way as to simulate what they have done in the past and what they would do in the job for which they are applying. For further details on this interviewing by simulation technique, pick up a copy of Lou Adler's *Hire With Your Head*.

A Real World Example of the Winning Formula: Waste Management

Many companies are just beginning to implement screening and assessment tools on a more formal basis. For years, the primary tool for making hiring decisions has been the interview, yet the research shows that the traditional interview fails miserably as a tool for making effective hires. It's almost impossible to give the same interview to every candidate who makes it past the first round of screening, so interview results are not an effective way to compare candidates. Further, interviews are, by their very nature, highly subjective and thus introduce the potential for non-job related factors to creep into an assessment. Hence, although interviews are a necessary part of every hiring process, some other form of assessment (such as the practices mentioned previously) should be administered to provide some balance.

One organization that is just beginning to explore the benefits of utilizing screening and assessment tools is Waste Management – a company formed from the "roll-up" of 1400 other companies. Today, Waste Management is a national organization with a total of 55,000 employees. The initiative is being lead by Dave Roberts, Director of Organizational Effectiveness, and Derrick Hamilton, Director of Recruitment, both of whom possess extensive backgrounds in HR consulting, including assessment, selection testing, and the development of training tools. They are in the early stages of implementing personality-based testing practices at Waste Management and have already seen measurable results.

Hamilton has implemented a program for the sales group within the organization. It begins with a skills/experience screen, which is followed by a behavioral interview.

Hiring managers have a set of pre-determined questions to use as an interviewing aid, thereby improving consistency and establishing benchmarks that can be used to predict the future success of hires made through the process. After this step is completed, a personality-based test is administered to help ensure a good fit. The intent is to prevent managers from making bad hires, while at the same time establishing consistency in the selection process. This would positively impact retention, turnover costs, and employee productivity. After just 8 months with this process in place, Waste Management sorted through over 8,000 applications to make 25 hires. Previously, Roberts says, these positions would have been given to a third-party search firm; the new process has thus enabled them to save 75% of the cost-per-hire. In addition, thanks to their ability to identify quality hires more precisely, he expects better productivity, increased retention, and significant cost savings.

Screening and assessment tools work best when a company has a clearly identified core culture. Since Waste Management has absorbed numerous smaller organizations from all over the country, establishing workplace cultural traits that the entire group has in common has not been easy. However, Roberts has identified two common threads, since starting with the company over a year ago:

- First, a "get it done" attitude; a determination to make things happen regardless of the obstacles in your path; and

- Second, the ability to work at a fast pace and with little time for perfecting interventions before they are implemented; in essence, problems are resolved and enhancements are made to programs while they are "live."

Having identified these cultural traits, Roberts and Hamilton now plan to introduce tests that will assess candidates for them. These tests will be implemented gradually and in a format that is designed to make the hiring manager's job an easy one.

Since much of the hiring at Waste Management is for light industrial and driving jobs, they hope to introduce voice-response and Internet-based screening tools that will make it easy for candidates to apply and be evaluated consistently, whether they are in New York, Houston, Los Angeles, or anyplace in between. To improve retention in this high-turnover area, Roberts and Hamilton have developed a strategy to "select for fundamental traits – things you can't change – then target our training dollars on the skills you CAN change." In support of this philosophy, Waste Management is focusing on identifying behaviors that correspond to the organization's core culture.

In addition to well-thought-out behavioral interviews, Roberts feels that the most successful screening and assessment tools are simulations and work samples. As noted earlier, simulations, though costly, are effective predictors of future success on-the-job. For positions that require specific skills (such as the many drivers employed by Waste Management), simulations are the best way to determine if a candidate's skills match the requirements of the job. Similarly, data from assessment centers show that work samples are the best predictors for future success on-the-job. Combined with behavioral interviewing to establish a candidate's culture fit, they provide a relatively reliable picture of the level of performance that a new hire will provide.

Chapter 5

Putting the Keys to Work

Now that you've got your sets of keys, it's time to unlock the doors to a truly world class recruiting and staffing function. The best way to do that is to follow Bernard Hodes Group's 360° process, that I described in Chapter 2. Its four-steps (Assess, Strategize, Implement, Measure) provide a structured way to put these powerful concepts into practice:

A. Assess

The first step to achieving world-class recruiting status is to accept the rule of thumb that the people you are looking for, probably aren't looking for you. Next, you need to perform an in-depth assessment of all aspects of your hiring process. Ideally, this audit should be performed by a highly-qualified third party. The purpose of the audit is to determine initial benchmarks that will serve as a road map for your journey to excellence. To be complete, the assessment should encompass a wide range of areas including:

1. **Requisition Management:** How many and what categories of requisitions are open now? How many have been filled within the last 12 months? How many requirements in each category do you anticipate over the next 12 months?

2. **Commitment to Talent:** How committed is top management to winning the War for Talent? How committed is your organization not only to recruiting the best, but to keeping and upgrading existing talent?

3. **Position as an Employer:** Why do people join your company? Why do they leave? Who's your competition? How do candidates view your organization as a potential employer?

4. **Culture:** How would you define your organization's culture? Is that definition what you'd like it to be? Are you aligning all staffing activities with the culture you seek to achieve?

5. **Hiring Process:** What are the plans and strategies for making the best hires in the shortest time, at the lowest cost? Who are the players in, and what are the components of, your hiring process? What level of satisfaction does this process produce among hiring managers as well as candidates?

6. **Technology:** Are you equipped with automated systems that combine state-of-the-art functionality with user friendliness? What are your expectations of technology – are you avoiding it, do you expect technology alone to do the vast majority of the work or do you have a more balanced view?

7. **Marketing Promotions:** What's your employment branding strategy? (If you have one!) Does it align with the company's overall product/services marketing message? Do you have a state-of-the-art career Web-site? What print, interactive and/or electronic advertising techniques do you utilize? How well are these various components working, and how consistent are your messages? Do you maintain a proactive

campaign, or just a reactive one? Do you have an active public relations effort dedicated to staffing?

8. **Metrics:** What do you measure? How accurate are your measurements? What would you like to measure? How do you stack up against the competition when it comes to cost, speed, candidate and new hire quality, and candidate and hiring manager satisfaction with your recruiting efforts?

Upon completion of your audit, you will have a report card that identifies where you stand and what you need to do to improve your organization. If your organization is like most – including even the best in the field – you'll conclude that you have a great deal of work to do. You may also need to call upon some outside expertise to help you answer questions brought up during the assessment.

B. Strategize (Key Set #1: Becoming an Employer of Choice)

It is probable that your assessment will reveal that your organization needs to formulate a game plan with which to achieve continuous improvement in a variety of areas.

To develop the plan, select your best and brightest contacts, internally and externally, and map out a course of action for accomplishing all of the following:

1. **Develop apostles through outstanding customer service**

   A staffing function is required to serve three customers: hiring managers, employees, and candidates. If any one of these groups becomes dissatisfied, the function's reputation and ability to perform its mission will suffer.

   - The hiring manager will go back to "doing his/her own thing;"

   - The candidate will find work elsewhere and never apply with your organization again; and

   - The employee will not recommend your organization to job prospects and/or will leave, adding additional burden to your workload.

   On the other hand, if your organization's customer service skills are outstanding enough to turn these three groups into "apostles," they'll literally do your job for you. All three groups will seek out talent and do the selling on your behalf.

2. Leverage the power of employer branding

How does one create the widely held view that Company A is a terrific place to work? By building a brand. A brand is a feeling, an aura, an image, an impression, a perception that becomes embedded through repetition, consistency, reinforcement, and confirmation, thereby becoming a reality. An employment brand centers around the creation of a great career Web-site. Such a site is highly visible and able to stand on its own, not as something six clicks removed from the home page on the general corporate site. This career area is where you "sell" your organization as an employer, spell out its opportunities, talk about its employees, list its jobs, and establish ongoing relationships with potential candidates. ALL of your marketing efforts should drive EVERY potential candidate to this Web-site.

3. Engage in market-driven behavior

Essentially, you need to treat candidates as customers. To do so, you must have staff and/or third party organizations capable of, and willing to:

- Be available at the candidate's convenience (evenings, weekends, whenever);

- Seek and sell rather than process and eliminate passive candidates; and

- Convince hiring managers to be more responsive and receptive to a "new breed" of candidate.

4. Formalize the staffing process through marketing and automation

Employers of choice are no longer paper-driven. They must be Internet-enabled and, to a large degree, automated. Systems and databases need to be set up and structured to permit candidate application and tracking from a wide variety of sources, including advertisements in any medium, resume mining and networking, employee referrals, internal mobility systems, career fairs, and third party submissions. Such automation produces valuable benefits, especially speed, efficiency, management reports, and metrics for improvement.

But automation, alone, will not be effective. It must be combined with the human touch of marketing, because recruiting remains a people business. Once potential candidates have been identified, they need to be pursued and "wooed" on an ongoing basis.

There is no one magic formula for building your brand as an employer. You need to use a mix of promotional outlets. No less important, you should measure the effectiveness of your recruitment marketing messages as well as your media selection so that you can determine which ones to emphasize, which ones to change, and which ones to eliminate.

Finally, your employment brand-building effort does not end when a potential candidate arrives at your Web-site. Reinforcement of your employer of choice message must occur throughout the entire hiring process. In fact, this continuous messaging is the one area that separates so-called employers of choice from true world-class recruiting organizations.

C. Implement

The purpose of the implementation process is to put all the information gathered during the first step, Assessment, to good use by utilizing the creativity resulting from the second step, Strategize. This is the point where you:

1. Complete and analyze your assessment to establish clear benchmarks, goals and projections.

2. Do your part to make Key Set #2, "The Cycle of Response and Responsiveness" work for you. Provide and position a team of talented individuals consisting of:

   • Project manager(s) dedicated to the success of your overall hiring process;

   • Project coordinators to work with hiring managers and candidates;

   • Cybrarians (Internet researchers);

- Marketing-oriented recruiters with various areas of expertise, who are available at the candidates' convenience (evenings, weekends, whenever);

- Recruitment marketing experts to develop creative and media strategies to fill the pipeline (resume database) even when requisitions aren't open;

- Programmers and IT support personnel to provide and maintain user-friendly technology; and

- Administrative personnel to ensure the overall efficiency of the process.

3. Use Key Set #3: "It's all in the marketing mix," to position and promote your organization as an employer of choice. By analyzing your culture, your competition, and how you are perceived as an employer, you can develop an appropriate branding strategy and implement it through an appropriate mix of marketing promotions. These promotions serve the purpose of driving traffic to a revamped, or newly-constructed, candidate-

friendly career site. This site, combined with appropriate technology, provides a high level of customer service to all participants in the hiring process.

4. Flexibility and hiring for a culture fit (Key Set #4) is the most complex of all of the key sets. As a first step, install and utilize technology that will get everyone on the same page. This coordination is best accomplished through the creation and implementation of a complex series of integrated Web-sites that provide different views and functionality for each of the main user groups: candidates, hiring managers, general employees, the Human Resource department, and third party organizations. Next, you'll need to install appropriate screening, interviewing and testing criteria that align with your culture.

5. Implement a hiring process, utilizing the best practices of all of the key sets previously described. This process should look like the diagram on the following page.

The Keys to Successful Recruiting and Staffing

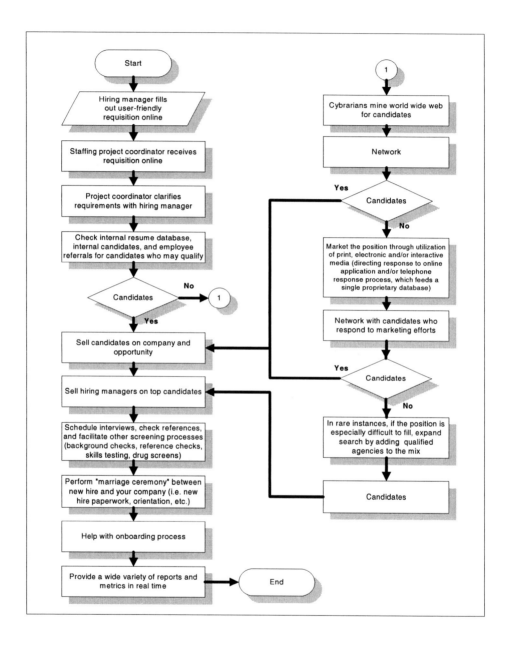

Start

Hiring manager fills out user-friendly requisition online

Staffing project coordinator receives requisition online

Project coordinator clarifies requirements with hiring manager

Check internal resume database, internal candidates, and employee referrals for candidates who may qualify

Candidates — No → 1

Yes

Sell candidates on company and opportunity

Sell hiring managers on top candidates

Schedule interviews, check references, and facilitate other screening processes (background checks, reference checks, skills testing, drug screens)

Perform "marriage ceremony" between new hire and your company (i.e. new hire paperwork, orientation, etc.)

Help with onboarding process

Provide a wide variety of reports and metrics in real time → End

1

Cybrarians mine world wide web for candidates

Network

Yes ← Candidates

No

Market the position through utilization of print, electronic and/or interactive media (directing response to online application and/or telephone response process, which feeds a single proprietary database)

Network with candidates who respond to marketing efforts

Yes ← Candidates

No

In rare instances, if the position is especially difficult to fill, expand search by adding qualified agencies to the mix

Candidates

D. Measure

At the Second Annual HR Partnership Summit on August 21, 2001, Robert W. Baird gave a presentation entitled "Emerging Platforms of Opportunity in Human Capital Management." He explained that "The war [for talent] is still hell.... Companies are rapidly awakening to the fact that they don't know how much they spend on their greatest asset [human capital], or much else about it."

Once again, the following are the four key components that should be measured in a world-class hiring process:

- QUALITY (of your hires)
- SATISFACTION (of participants in the hiring process)
- TIME (required to fill open positions)
- COST (incurred in the recruiting process as well as cost of mediocre hires and attrition).

However, it is important to consider the following comment by Nick Burkholder, the founder of Staffing.org, an organization dedicated to establishing "benchmarks" for the staffing industry: "We've always noted that the first absolute of any high performance organization is to establish the right, measurable objectives — and benchmarking is invariably deleterious to that."[32]

Although it may, at first, appear paradoxical, Nick is not alone in his thinking. In March of 2002, at a Human Resource Planning Society Conference in Chicago, a couple of noted speakers suggested that it's time to stop benchmarking and to start focusing on organization solutions:

- Len Schlesinger, COO of The Limited, called for HR executives to address their missions and "not how other people do their jobs."
- Core competency expert C.K. Prahalad pointed out that one's own enterprise and its problems "should be the starting point for useful HR work."

What these experts are saying, and what I endorse, is that while it's very important to measure and continuously improve on your own organization's performance, you must avoid dwelling on comparisons that pit your organization's results against those of other staffing functions. There are just too many variables and inconsistencies involved to arrive at any accurate and valid "tales of the tape."

Einstein once said that the idea is to "make things simple, not simpler." I've tried to make navigating the road to world class recruiting sound simple, but the journey is complex and difficult. I feel compelled to state, once again, that staffing is essentially a people business. Wherever there are people, there are personality conflicts coupled with skepticism and resistance to change. So, no matter how well you've done your assessment, strategy, implementation, and measurement, your efforts will fail without the preparation, flexibility and willingness to navigate your way through the obstacles ahead. Improvement or "tweaking" is all about doing anything and everything to secure hiring manager buy-in for what you're trying to accomplish. It involves a great deal of patience, communication, change management, motivation, customer service, and training. This area is where your commitment, and that of top management, will be most severely tested.

My final message, therefore, is an exhortation to be strong in the face of this testing. What we do is critical to the survival and ultimate prosperity of the enterprise. Despite the skeptics, the problems, the challenges along the way, we can always be confident of that. The staffing mission is a vital one, and that is the best justification I know for the courage and commitment we must show.

On the other hand, let's all acknowledge that it's O.K. to have some fear about venturing into what, for many of us, will be uncharted waters. Certainly, undertaking the initiatives I've described will involve battling with the status quo, and victory cannot be assured. After all, "if winning were easy, everyone would do it." It's not a coincidence that this is also the title of a book of quotations by Kim Doren and Charlie Jones.

A Winning Formula

One of my favorite athletes is the tennis great, Boris Becker. When talking about what it takes to win, he once said, "I drew my strength from fear. Fear of losing. I don't remember the games I won, only the games I lost."[33]

May this approach enable you to be as successful in building your world class recruiting and staffing organization as Boris Becker was in conquering the world class field of tennis players at Wimbledon three times.

Afterword

More on Metrics

Why More On Metrics?

Upon completion of this book, I passed the final draft around to industry friends and trusted colleagues. A number of them felt that while I had sufficiently covered the first three elements of the Hodes 360 process (Assess, Strategize and Implement), I could and should say more about the final and perhaps most important element: Measure. So, that's what I'm going to do in this Chapter. For our purposes here, I'm going to define Measure as a staffing function's use of all appropriate metrics. With that definition in mind, let's take a look at the metrics of staffing.

The language of business is numbers, and metrics are the means by which the staffing function translates its work into that language. While this translation is clearly important, however, it is not the ultimate purpose of metrics. Numerical measurements are tools, not ends. Hence, the reason for investing in and using metrics is to do something with them, and that something is performance improvement. It is not to evaluate what's done and stop, but rather, to use the insights that come out of that evaluation to enhance results. Whether the scope of a metrics program is broad or targeted, the goal should always be to augment the value of the staffing function to the enterprise. To put it another way, the role of metrics in recruiting is not audit, but excellence.

In today's tough business climate, every unit of the enterprise must perform at peak levels, and all units must make a tangible contribution to its economic goals. The use of metrics enables the staffing function to meet both of those requirements. They help staffing managers oversee staffing activities and ensure their optimum performance, and they detail the contribution of those activities to the organization's success. In essence, using metrics provides discipline in staffing operations and clarity in staffing communications, a way to achieve success and a way to communicate the value of that success to senior enterprise leaders. At the bottom line, they open the window on the strategic contribution staffing makes to the enterprise.

Metrics, however, also have a tactical role. They provide a first step – a place to start in a performance improvement campaign. When properly installed, they give an organization both a quantified description of its baseline operating level and subsequent measures of the progress being made to enhance that performance. Because the metrics are consistent in definition and application, they offer a reliable and insightful gauge of initiatives to upgrade the efficiency, productivity, and quality of staffing programs and services. They are the signposts by which the staffing function determines which direction(s) to take to:

- align the staffing model with the business model of the enterprise;

- optimize staffing effectiveness in and contribution to enterprise operations; and

- create a real and sustainable financial impact in the business of the enterprise.

To achieve those goals, however, metrics must be embedded within a well-designed and carefully implemented process. This process begins by collecting data that accurately and meaningfully measure an organization's performance. These data must then be reduced and transformed into information that portrays how effectively and efficiently work is being accomplished and how useful that work is to the enterprise. This information only becomes worthwhile knowledge, however, when it is analyzed and acted upon to make better decisions and improve performance. In other words, without analysis, metrics are useless. And without follow up actions based on that analysis, they are a waste of time.

What Should Metrics Measure?
(How do you best fill your "CUP?")

Optimally, a metrics program should measure the staffing function's performance in three areas that are easily remembered by the acronym C-U-P:

Contribution: The staffing function's assistance to the enterprise.

How good are the products and services recruiters provide to the enterprise? This area of measurement focuses on the output of the staffing function: the candidates that are sourced and hired and the caliber of service that is provided to hiring managers and to candidates. Here, the appropriate metric is quality-of-hire, as indicated by (a) post-hire performance appraisal scores and/or the accomplishment of pre-set, near-term goals, and (b) service ratings by hiring managers, new hires and other candidates.

Utilization: The staffing function's management of enterprise assets.

How well does recruiting oversee the assets in its charge – the talent database(s) and recruitment Web-site(s) of the enterprise? This area of measurement evaluates the return on investments made in these assets and, as a consequence, their value to the enterprise. Hence, such metrics as the percentage of positions filled from the database or Web-site and the offer-to-acceptance ratio among candidates sourced from those assets are appropriate metrics.

<u>P</u>roductivity: The staffing function's use of enterprise resources.

How well have recruiters and staffing managers used the organization's people, process, tools and technology to accomplish their work? In essence, this area of measurement focuses on the efficiency and productivity of recruiting operations. Among appropriate metrics are the source that originally directed each candidate to the Web-site, cost-per-hire and time-to-fill or cycle time.

For best results, an organization should design its metrics program to address all three of these areas. This approach generates the consistent stream of data-information-knowledge that leads to comprehensive, in-depth improvements in total recruiting performance. Realistically, however, it may not be feasible or practical for an organization to launch its metrics program with such a broad scope. Indeed, its decision to install metrics in any one or all of these areas as well as its selection of the metric or metrics it will use within any single area must be based on the organization's readiness for measurement (its culture and resources) and its measurement capabilities (its data collection and analysis processes).

There is no one-size-fits-all approach to metrics, so successful installation depends upon an organization's ability to balance its desire to use metrics with its current capacity to do so. Whatever the scope – whether it's a broad gauged metrics program or a more targeted initiative – the use of metrics is beneficial as long as it is based on careful assessment and tailored implementation.

How Do You Begin?

For some time now, there has been much debate over which metrics provide the best portrait of an organization's recruiting operations. Some champion quantitative measures of efficiency, such as cost-per-hire and time-to-fill. Others believe that qualitative metrics, such as offer-to-acceptance ratio and client satisfaction scores, represent more accurate and useful gauges of performance. This issue not only consumes a great deal of time and attention, it diverts our attention from the key issue.

Metrics cannot simply be bolted onto an organization as an afterthought. The beginning point in adopting metrics in any organization should be assessment. What must be done by the organization to prepare its culture and process for measurement? Once that preparation has been completed, it should then guide the organization's selection, definition, implementation and use of metrics. In other words, how an organization begins the use of metrics – the foundation it builds via its assessment and preparation – are the true determinants of the ultimate success of its metrics effort.

Metrics programs need not be elaborate or broad in scope. They must be well conceived, however, because they can actually hurt a staffing function when they are not. Indeed, poorly designed and/or executed metrics programs can have any of a number of serious consequences:

- Waste of Financial Resources. Dysfunctional cultures and/or sub-optimized measurement processes can cost a lot of money without providing a meaningful return on that investment (i.e., the ability to identify, plan for, and implement operating improvements).

- Diminished Productivity. Such cultures and processes can also consume inordinate amounts of staff and management time and attention without yielding tangible results (i.e., genuine performance improvements and the ability to describe those gains effectively to senior leaders in the enterprise).

- Loss of Credibility. Failure to consider cultural constraints and/or poorly designed or implemented measurement processes can generate data that are inaccurate, misunderstood or mistrusted by senior leaders in the enterprise and, as a consequence, undermine faith in and support for the staffing function and its managers.

To avoid these pitfalls, Bernard Hodes Group (Hodes) has developed a multi-step methodology for the installation of metrics programs. This methodology provides a methodical and complete guide to the decisions that must be made and the actions that must be taken to bring metrics into an organization successfully. It is based on Hodes' proven 360° formula that I've described in earlier chapters of this book.

The Hodes Metrics Methodology™ consists of four steps as described below:

Step 1: Assess

This step seeks to determine an organization's objective state and its current ability to achieve that goal. First, what are the outcomes the organization expects the staffing function to deliver? What level of performance do the customers of the staffing function want? Second, how does the staffing function work to achieve the objective state? What actions does it take, what information does it acquire or generate, and how are the actions and information flows sequenced to produce those outcomes?

To be truly effective, metrics programs must be designed to optimize the building blocks of staffing performance. What are those building blocks? They are:

- **People:** the internal and external talent relationships within the organization as well as its commitment to talent, its market position as an employer and its culture.

- **Process:** the organization's procedures for requirements identification and management, sourcing, interviewing, assessment, selection, and offer formulation as well as its procedures for new hire assimilation and employee development and retention.

- **Tools:** the organization's employment brand and brand communications program (including its career Web-site) as well as its sourcing, recruiting and retention strategies, budget, priority and resources.

- **Technology:** the organization's engine that manages jobs on and response from its recruitment Web-site, as well as its resume management system and database.

The improvement of recruiting operations can only be achieved by optimizing these four elements. Indeed, doing so is the only viable strategy by which an organization can install a world class staffing function. It is important, however, to focus on those operations (i.e., activities, information flows, decision-making) that meet two very important criteria: First, the operations must have a real and substantial impact on the organization's success, and second, the staffing function must have meaningful control over the conduct of the operations. While there are many different recruiting operations that can be gauged by one metric or another, only measurements of operations that satisfy these two criteria will be both useful to staffing managers and credible in the enterprise at large.

The output of this step should be a clear understanding of both what's expected of the staffing function by its customers (i.e., the definition of success) and its current deployment of resources to accomplish that objective (i.e., its operational baseline).

Step 2: Strategize

This step determines the optimum metrics for a specific organization. In other words, what measures best describe the staffing function's performance in delivering the desired outcomes or objective state, identified in Step 1? And, which definition of each of those measures seems most reasonable to the organization. For example, in the calculation of cost-per-hire, what cost elements should be included and which should be excluded?

Hodes believes that the selection of a specific metric or metrics must be based on two key principles:

Principle 1: If the metrics fit, use them.

Many organizations never implement metrics programs because they are unable to find metrics that can pass the same tests of rigor as those applied to metrics in the world of finance. Despite decades of research among experts in academia and the accounting field, there are still no generally accepted procedures for quantifying operations in the HR department, in general, and the staffing function, in particular. While certain staffing metrics, such as cost-per-hire, have the look and feel of financial metrics, the fact remains that there are no standards for measuring staffing performance that would enable the results to pass the tests of validity required to appear on a balance sheet or income statement.

This search for financial similarity, however, is a red herring. It prevents the staffing function from implementing metrics programs, yet has no bearing on their success. Staffing metrics need not reach the same high bar of rigor as that imposed on financial measures because staffing metrics have a different purpose. While financial metrics must be able to support an audit of an organization's business performance, metrics in the staffing function must be able to identify and scope potential improvements in the way work gets done. Hence, the standard for selecting the staffing metrics to be used in a measurement process is not absolute validity (as required in finance), but face validity. In other words, the metrics that are selected by an organization must produce data that seem reasonable and credible to those in the staffing function and its customer base who will use them.

That level of general acceptance is sufficient to support the initial installation of the measurement process. Subsequent iterations of the process will then provide the necessary experiential-based insight to refine the initial metric selections, their definitions and/or the procedures for data collection, reduction and use. Hence, Hodes adheres to a strategy of "progressive sufficiency" which enables an organization to begin with what it knows (or believes) to be true and then to upgrade that knowledge based on what it learns. It is a practical and valid way to get started on measuring recruiting operations for performance improvement.

Principle 2: Use the metrics that best fill your own organization's specific "CUP."

Recruiting metrics must be tailored to the organization that will use them. There is a wide (and growing) range of metrics that can be used by an organization to measure the performance of operations in its staffing function. These include:

Contribution: The staffing function's assistance to the enterprise

Ratio of fill to openings or requirements

Average number of days openings remain unfilled

Quality-of-Hire

      Percentage match with specified requirements

      Post-hire performance appraisal scores

      Retention

Cost of mediocre hires

Cost of vacancies

Client (hiring manager) satisfaction

Candidate satisfaction (selected and not selected)

Utilization: The staffing function's management of enterprise assets

Return on asset

Percent fill from talent database

Percent fill from recruitment Web-site

Percent fill from internal mobility database

Percent fill from employee referral program

Return on investment

Savings generated by sourcing from talent database, recruitment Web-site, internal mobility database, and employee referral program

Rather than with additional advertising

Rather than by using third party sources

Monetized value of time saved by sourcing from talent database, recruitment Web-site, internal mobility database, and employee referral program

Productivity: The staffing function's use of enterprise resources

Cycle time

Time-to-submit (candidates to a hiring manager)

Percentage of candidates screened-in for further

assessment

Cost-per-candidate

Cost-per-qualified candidate

Cost-per-hire

Channel optimization

       Cost-per-qualified candidate by channel

       Cost-per-hire by channel

       Total yield by channel (quantity and quality)

       Diversity yield by channel (quantity and quality)

       Candidate retention by channel

       Interview-to-offer ratio among candidates by channel

       Offer-to-acceptance ratio among candidates by channel

       Percentage of candidates screened-in for further assessment by channel

There is no one set of these metrics that is appropriate for all organizations. Indeed, the selection of metrics is a culture-specific exercise. It must be based on an organization's:

- readiness for measurement (i.e., the commitment to metrics and their priority at senior leadership, middle management and user levels);

- knowledge of measurement (i.e., the training in and experience with staffing metrics at senior leadership, middle management and user levels);

- historical experience with staffing metrics (i.e., have metrics been used in the past and, if so, what was the result);

- technological capacity to collect and store data accurately and efficiently; and

- financial capacity to support data collection, reduction and use.

In essence, the metrics an organization chooses to use must be tailored to its situational reality. The selection of metrics based on anything else, including the experience of peer organizations and simplistic "metrics in a box" programs, is almost certain to fail and, in the process, to cause disruption and even performance degradation in the staffing function.

Step 3: Implement

The successful implementation of a metrics program begins with the design of its information sub-structure. Where will the data be collected and stored? Who will analyze the data and transform it into information and on what schedule will that transformation be accomplished? To whom will the information be sent and what will they do with it? And equally as important, what resources will be required to support the total effort?

The goal is to determine where, in the staffing function's actions and information flows (the baseline identified in Step 1), the organization can efficiently and unobtrusively collect the data it needs for the metrics it selected (in Step 2). It must also assess what financial, staff, training, systems, time, organizational development and other resources will be required to integrate the information substructure into the organization's way of doing business.

To be most effective, a metrics program must have an information substructure that incorporates the following elements:

- A data collection facility at the appropriate point(s) in recruiting operations;

- A storage and retrieval capability for the data that are collected;

- A data reduction capability for the calculation of the metric(s); and

- A communications protocol to identify who in the organization will receive which metrics and how.

Step 4: Measure

Finally, the performance improvement superstructure must be designed. How will the information provided by the metrics be used to:

(a) evaluate performance in the operational areas selected in Step 1;

(b) identify and assess potential improvement initiatives; and

(c) select specific initiatives for implementation and evaluation?

Who will be responsible for these actions and what resources will be required to support them?

The best design for a performance improvement superstructure is one with a closed-loop that incorporates the following activities:

- Regular review (monthly, quarterly and annually) of the metrics data and analysis of their meaning;

- Identification and assessment of alternative initiatives that could be undertaken in areas where metrics data indicate either the need or opportunity for performance improvement (i.e., "what if" analyses);

- Implementation of the selected improvement initiative(s). In most cases, performance improvement is most efficiently achieved through iterative change. This approach begins with the selection and installation of a single initiative while holding all other activities constant so as to get a true measure of its impact. Once that impact has been evaluated, optimized and installed, or eliminated, a new initiative can be selected and managed in the same way.

- Collection of data measuring the impact of selected initiatives (from Step 3) and input of that data to Step 1 above.

So, What's the Bottom Line?

Making staffing metrics happen in an enterprise isn't easy. Despite all of the hype about their promise, metrics programs cannot be effectively integrated into an organization unless they meet several critical preconditions. First, the organization must recognize what metrics can and should do for it. Second, the organization must have or acquire a realistic sense of what's involved in its adoption and use of metrics. And third, the organization must proceed through a logical and comprehensive approach that will accomplish and sustain both its shift to a measurement culture and its effective use of a measurement process. The Hodes Metrics Methodology™ satisfies these preconditions and, as a consequence, brings metrics – useful measurements of recruiting performance – into the reach of every organization.

The next step, then, is to get started. In today's War for the Best Talent, there is no more important initiative than the optimization of your staffing function. There is no better time than the present to begin. But in implementing your metrics program, as well as any of the keys to successful recruiting and staffing, don't hesitate to call upon experts in the field to help you add value and achieve meaningful, lasting and credible results.

ENDNOTES

[1] Harris, Jim and Brannick, Joan: *"Finding and Keeping Great Employees,"* (New York, AMACOM, 1999), Preface p. XI

[2] Towers Perrin Talent Report: *"New Realities in Today's Workforce,"* 2001, Executive Summary available at http://towers.com

[3] Towers Perrin Talent Report: *"New Realities in Today's Workforce,"* 2001, Executive Summary available at http://towers.com

[4] Wheeler, Kevin:, Periodic Potpourri: *"The First Set of Results,"* Electronic Recruiting Exchange, April 24, 2002, http://www.erexchange.com/

[5] Success in Recruiting and Retaining, *"Your Competitors are Ready to Hire,"* National Institute of Business Management, July, 2002, http://www.nibm.net

[6] Harris, Jim and Brannick, Joan: *"Finding and Keeping Great Employees,"* (New York, AMACOM, 1999), p. 7

[7] Watson Wyatt, *"Work USA 2000, Employee Commitment and the Bottom Line,"* www.watsonwyatt.com

[8] Buckingham, Marcus and Coffman, Curt: *"First Break All the Rules,"* (New York, Simon & Schuster, 1999) p. 33

[9] Heskett, James; Sasser, W. Earl; and Schlesinger, Leonard: *"The Service Profit Chain,"* (New York, The Free press, 1997) p. 11

[10] BNA, Inc, *"Weak Economy Brings Sharp Decline in Employee Turnover, BNA Survey Finds,"* BNA Survey, March 14, 2002, http://www.bna.com/BNA/press/2002/worksurv2.htm

[11] Staffing.org, *"Staffing Metrics Benchmark Report,"* (Willow Grove, PA, Staffing.org, 2002) p. 11, website: http://staffing.org

[12] McKenna, Patrick and Maister, David, *"First Among Equals,"* (New York, THE FREE PRESS, 2002) p. 155-156

[13] Bliss, Bill, *"Cost of Turnover,"* Bliss & Associates, Inc., 2001 http://www.blissassociates.com/html/articles/cost_of_turnover15.html

[14] Sullivan, Dr. John, *"Instead of the Cost of Hire...Measure the Cost of a Bad Hire,"* erdaily, Electronic Recruiting Exchange, Feb 5, 1999, http://www.erexchange.com

[15] Harris, Jim and Brannick, Joan: *"Finding and Keeping Great Employees,"* (New York, AMACOM, 1999), p. 12

[16] Tulgan, Bruce, *"Promoting Custom Career Paths,"* erdaily, Electronic Recruiting Exchange, 10/12/01, http://www.erexchange.com

[17] Tulgan, Bruce, "*Promoting Custom Career Paths,*" erdaily, Electronic Recruiting Exchange, 10/12/01, http://www.erexchange.com

[18] SHRM Workplace Visions Newsletter, "*The Telecommuting Explosion,*" April 29, 2002

[19] Sullivan, Dr. John, "*The 'Big Secret': Top Performers Are a Bargain,*" erdaily, Electronic Recruiting Exchange, 4/29/02, http://www.erexchange.com

[20] Maister, David, "*Employer Values,*" presented at Senior Management Program, Omnicom University, July, 2000.

[21] Tulgan, Bruce, "*Winning the Talent Wars,*" (New York, W.W. Norton & Company, Inc., 2001) p. 156

[22] Deal, Terrence and Kennedy, Allan: "*Corporate Cultures,*" (Cambridge, PERSEUS, 2000) intro p. IV

[23] Deal, Terrence and Kennedy, Allan: "*Corporate Cultures,*" (Cambridge, PERSEUS, 2000) p. 16

[24] Harris, Jim and Brannick, Joan: "*Finding and Keeping Great Employees*" (New York, AMACOM, 1999), Preface XIV

[25] Harris, Jim and Brannick, Joan: "*Finding and Keeping Great Employees*" (New York, AMACOM, 1999), Preface XI-XII

[26] Tulgan, Bruce, "*Recruiting the Workforce of the Future,*" (HRD Press), 2000, p. 22-23

[27] Adler, Lou, "Hire With Your Head," (Hoboken, NJ, John Wiley & Sons, Inc) p. 26

[28] Adler, Lou, "Hire With Your Head," (Hoboken, NJ, John Wiley & Sons, Inc), p. 89

[29] Adler, Lou, "Hire With Your Head," (Hoboken, NJ, John Wiley & Sons, Inc), p. 23

[30] Wheeler, Kevin; Foss, Erik; and Handler, Dr. Charles: "*Screening and Assessment: Best Practices,*" Global Learning Resources, Inc., Fall 2001, p. 24, http://www.glresources.com

[31] Wheeler, Kevin; Foss, Erik; and Handler, Dr. Charles: "*Screening and Assessment: Best Practices,*" Global Learning Resources, Inc. report, p. 24, http://www.glresources.com

[32] Burkholder, Nick, "*eBulletin,*" April 5, 2002, HR Engineer, Willowgrove, PA, http://www.hrengineer.com

[33] Doren, Kim and Jones, Charlie, "If Winning Were Easy, Everyone Would Do It," (Andrews McNeel Publishing, Kansas City, 2002) p. 43